most loved recipe collection

# most loved

# Festive Baking

**Pictured on front cover:**

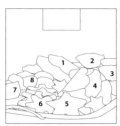

1. Festive Fruitcake, page 6
2. Butter Tarts, page 74
3. Cranapple Tarts, page 72
4. Stollen, page 112
5. Gingerbread Stars, page 30
6. Brown Sugar And Spice, page 46
7. Fruit And Honey Bars, page 56
8. Santa's Whiskers, page 45

**Pictured on back cover:**

1. Butterscotch Shortbread, page 32
2. Shortbread, page 32

**Most Loved Festive Baking**

Copyright © Company's Coming Publishing Limited

All rights reserved worldwide. No part of this book may be reproduced, stored in a retrieval system or transmitted in any form by any means without written permission in advance from the publisher.

In the case of photocopying or other reprographic copying, a license may be purchased from the Canadian Copyright Licensing Agency (Access Copyright). Visit www.accesscopyright.ca or call toll free 1-800-893-5777. In the United States, please contact the Copyright Clearance Centre at www.copyright.com or call 978-646-8600.

Brief portions of this book may be reproduced for review purposes, provided credit is given to the source. Reviewers are invited to contact the publisher for additional information.

First Printing November 2008

Library and Archives Canada Cataloguing in Publication

Paré, Jean, date-
Most loved festive baking / by Jean Paré.
(Most loved recipe collection)
Includes indexes.
ISBN 978-1-897069-67-7
1. Christmas cookery. 2. Baking. I. Title. II. Series: Paré, Jean, date-
Most loved recipe collection.
TX763.P37 2008            641.5'686            C2008-902011-1

Published by
**Company's Coming Publishing Limited**
2311 – 96 Street
Edmonton, Alberta, Canada T6N 1G3
Tel: 780-450-6223   Fax: 780-450-1857
www.companyscoming.com

Company's Coming is a registered trademark owned by Company's Coming Publishing Limited

We acknowledge the financial support of the Government of Canada through the Book Publishing Industry Development Program (BPIDP) for our publishing activities.

Printed in China

We gratefully acknowledge the following suppliers for their generous support of our Test and Photography Kitchens:

Broil King Barbecues
Corelle®
Hamilton Beach® Canada
Lagostina®
Proctor Silex® Canada
Tupperware®

Our special thanks to the following businesses for providing props for photography:

Danesco Inc.
Emile Henry
Corningware®
Pfaltzgraff Canada
Winners Stores
The Bay
Pier 1 Imports
Totally Bamboo
Casa Bugatti
Cherison Enterprises Inc.
Klass Works

**Pictured from left:** Gingerbread Stars, page 30; Cherry Strudel Dessert, page 24; Turtle Cheesecake, page 10; Chinese Chews, page 59

# table of contents

*"Never share a recipe you wouldn't use yourself"*

# the Company's Coming story

Jean Paré (pronounced "jeen PAIR-ee") grew up understanding that the combination of family, friends and home cooking is the best recipe for a good life. From her mother, she learned to appreciate good cooking, while her father praised even her earliest attempts in the kitchen. When Jean left home, she took with her a love of cooking, many family recipes and an intriguing desire to read cookbooks as if they were novels!

When her four children had all reached school age, Jean volunteered to cater the 50th anniversary celebration of the Vermilion School of Agriculture, now Lakeland College, in Alberta, Canada. Working out of her home, Jean prepared a dinner for more than 1,000 people, launching a flourishing catering operation that continued for over 18 years. During that time, she had countless opportunities to test new ideas with immediate feedback—resulting in empty plates and contented customers! Whether preparing cocktail sandwiches for a house party or serving a hot meal for 1,500 people, Jean Paré earned a reputation for great food, courteous service and reasonable prices.

As requests for her recipes increased, Jean was often asked the question, "Why don't you write a cookbook?" Jean responded by teaming up with her son, Grant Lovig, in the fall of 1980 to form Company's Coming Publishing Limited. The publication of *150 Delicious Squares* on April 14, 1981 marked the debut of what would soon become one of the world's most popular cookbook series.

The company has grown since those early days when Jean worked from a spare bedroom in her home. Today, she continues to write recipes while working closely with the staff of the Recipe Factory, as the Company's Coming test kitchen is affectionately known. There she fills the role of mentor, assisting with the development of recipes people most want to use for everyday cooking and easy entertaining. Every Company's Coming recipe is kitchen-tested before it is approved for publication.

Jean's daughter, Gail Lovig, is responsible for marketing and distribution, leading a team that includes sales personnel located in major cities across Canada. Company's Coming cookbooks are distributed in Canada, the United States, Australia and other world markets. Bestsellers many times over in English, Company's Coming cookbooks have also been published in French and Spanish.

Familiar and trusted in home kitchens around the world, Company's Coming cookbooks are offered in a variety of formats. Highly regarded as kitchen workbooks, the softcover Original Series, with its lay-flat plastic comb binding, is still a favourite among readers.

Jean Paré's approach to cooking has always called for quick and easy recipes using everyday ingredients. That view has served her well. The recipient of many awards, including the Queen Elizabeth Golden Jubilee Medal, Jean was appointed Member of the Order of Canada, her country's highest lifetime achievement honour.

Jean continues to gain new supporters by adhering to what she calls The Golden Rule of Cooking: *Never share a recipe you wouldn't use yourself.* It's an approach that has worked—millions of times over!

# foreword

The holiday season is a time for joyous celebration and spending time with loved ones—and for enjoying good things to eat. Serving up holiday cheer is a must when friends and family gather together, and nothing says holiday cheer like delicious baked goods.

Whether you're hosting a grand dinner party, Christmas morning brunch or a simple afternoon tea, baking is an important part of the festivities. You'll need cookies and squares, a fruitcake for tradition and fresh-baked rolls to serve with cheese. In these pages, you'll find plenty of festive favourites, as well as new recipes that are sure to become holiday traditions in your family.

Everyone knows that time has a way of disappearing during the holidays. Planning ahead will let you spend more time with your nearest and dearest than you do in the kitchen. Make a list of your family's favourites ahead of time, then choose a few new recipes to try. Since many baked items can be stored in the freezer for at least a month, plan to use November for baking and leave December for holiday cheer. Also, if you need a last-minute hostess gift, just wrap up some of your pre-made biscotti or muffins to share with those you'll be visiting over the season.

Along with delicious recipes, we've provided sidebars with helpful tips for simplifying your holiday baking, as well as interesting information on ingredients and some of your favourite Christmas songs, stories, traditions and treats. For even more fun, you can share these tidbits of holiday trivia with your family and friends over coffee and dessert.

This Christmas, fill your home with the warm scents and sweet flavours of our favourite festive baked goods—they're sure to become your favourites too. With *Most Loved Festive Baking*, sharing the joy of the season has never been easier, or more delicious.

*Jean Paré*

## nutrition information

Each recipe is analyzed using the most current version of the Canadian Nutrient File from Health Canada, which is based on the United States Department of Agriculture (USDA) Nutrient Database.

- If more than one ingredient is listed (such as "butter or hard margarine"), or if a range is given (1 – 2 tsp., 5 – 10 mL), only the first ingredient or first amount is analyzed.

- For meat, poultry and fish, the serving size per person is based on the recommended 4 oz. (113 g) uncooked weight (without bone), which is 2 – 3 oz. (57 – 85 g) cooked weight (without bone)—approximately the size of a deck of playing cards.

- Milk used is 1% M.F. (milk fat), unless otherwise stated.

- Cooking oil used is canola oil, unless otherwise stated.

- Ingredients indicating "sprinkle," "optional," or "for garnish" are not included in the nutrition information.

- The fat in recipes and combination foods can vary greatly depending on the sources and types of fats used in each specific ingredient. For these reasons, the amount of saturated, monounsaturated and polyunsaturated fats may not add up to the total fat content.

Vera C. Mazurak, Ph.D.
Nutritionist

*Everyone will be a fruitcake lover once they try this rich, dark cake studded with jewel-coloured bits of fruit. This recipe makes four cakes, so you'll have enough on hand to get through the holiday season.*

## about fruitcake

This dense, fruit-filled cake became a Christmas tradition in the eighteenth century, when dried fruits would only be eaten on holidays and special occasions. Despite its history as the ultimate in festive luxury, some people aren't overly fond of fruitcake. If you have friends or family who have been turned off to fruitcake, this may be your year to convert them into fruitcake lovers after sampling a slice of a really good homemade one.

# Festive Fruitcake

| | | |
|---|---|---|
| Raisins | 4 lbs. | 1.8 kg |
| Chopped mixed glazed fruit | 2 lbs. | 900 g |
| Currants | 1 lb. | 454 g |
| Red glazed cherries | 1 lb. | 454 g |
| Jar of maraschino cherries, drained | 16 oz. | 500 mL |
| Chopped pitted dates | 1/2 lb. | 225 g |
| All-purpose flour | 1 cup | 250 mL |
| Butter (or hard margarine), softened | 1 lb. | 454 g |
| Granulated sugar | 2 cups | 500 mL |
| Egg yolks (large) | 12 | 12 |
| Can of crushed pineapple (with juice) | 14 oz. | 398 mL |
| Vanilla extract | 1 tbsp. | 15 mL |
| All-purpose flour | 2 1/4 cups | 550 mL |
| Cocoa, sifted if lumpy | 4 tsp. | 20 mL |
| Ground cinnamon | 4 tsp. | 20 mL |
| Baking powder | 1 tbsp. | 15 mL |
| Ground nutmeg | 2 tsp. | 10 mL |
| Salt | 1 tsp. | 5 mL |
| Baking soda | 1/2 tsp. | 2 mL |
| Orange (or apple) juice | 1 cup | 250 mL |
| Chopped walnuts | 1 lb. | 454 g |
| Egg whites (large), room temperature | 12 | 12 |

Line four 9 x 5 x 3 inch (22 x 12.5 x 7.5 cm) loaf pans with greased foil. Set aside. Stir first 7 ingredients in extra-large bowl until coated with flour. Set aside.

Cream butter and sugar in large bowl. Add egg yolks, 3 at a time, beating well after each addition. Add pineapple and vanilla extract. Stir.

Combine next 7 ingredients in medium bowl.

Add flour mixture to butter mixture in 3 additions, alternating with orange juice in 2 additions, stirring well after each addition until just combined. Add walnuts. Stir.

*(continued on next page)*

1. Dundee Cake, page 9
2. Festive Fruitcake, above
3. Favourite Fruitcake, page 8

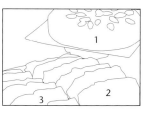

Using clean beaters, beat egg whites in separate large bowl until stiff peaks form. Fold into batter. Fold in fruit mixture. Spread in prepared pans. Bake in 275°F (140°C) oven for about 3 hours until wooden pick inserted in centre comes out clean. Let stand in pan on wire rack until completely cooled. Makes 4 fruitcakes, about 3 3/4 lbs. (1.7 kg) each. Each cake cuts into 16 slices, for a total of 64 slices.

*1 slice: 337 Calories; 11.6 g Total Fat (2.6 g Mono, 3.8 g Poly, 4.4 g Sat); 51 mg Cholesterol; 59 g Carbohydrate; 3 g Fibre; 4 g Protein; 134 mg Sodium*

Pictured on front cover and below.

*A fruitcake that's sure to please everyone, this one's not too dark and not too light. Make and freeze these cakes a few weeks ahead and you'll have more time to spend with your friends and family during the holidays.*

## fruitcake tips

1. Prepare the loaf pan and all the ingredients before you start.

2. Sift the dry ingredients so they can be thoroughly incorporated throughout the fruitcake.

3. Fruitcakes bake for a significantly longer time than most cakes. Lining the pan with foil or several layers of parchment paper ensures that the cake cooks evenly without forming a hard, thick crust. If you're lining the pan with parchment paper, be sure to grease the pan and between each layer to hold the paper in place.

4. Bake fruitcakes slowly in a low-temperature oven. If it's too hot, the cake will crack and form a hard crust.

5. Fruitcakes typically sit in a cool place for a few weeks before serving in order to develop their full flavour. Be sure to remove the foil or parchment paper and wrap with plastic wrap before storing. Often the fruitcake is wrapped in cheesecloth that has been first soaked with liqueur during the "aging" process.

# Favourite Fruitcake

| | | |
|---|---|---|
| Golden raisins | 1 lb. | 454 g |
| Chopped glazed pineapple | 3/4 lb. | 340 g |
| Red glazed cherries | 3/4 lb. | 340 g |
| Diced mixed peel | 1/2 lb. | 225 g |
| Pecan halves | 4 oz. | 113 g |
| Whole blanched almonds, halved | 4 oz. | 113 g |
| All-purpose flour | 1/2 cup | 125 mL |
| Butter (or hard margarine), softened | 1 cup | 250 mL |
| Brown sugar, packed | 2 cups | 500 mL |
| Large eggs | 4 | 4 |
| All-purpose flour | 2 1/2 cups | 625 mL |
| Baking powder | 1 tsp. | 5 mL |
| Ground cinnamon | 1 tsp. | 5 mL |
| Salt | 1 tsp. | 5 mL |
| Instant coffee granules | 1 tbsp. | 15 mL |
| Hot water | 1 tbsp. | 15 mL |
| Apple jelly | 1/2 cup | 125 mL |
| Milk | 1/2 cup | 125 mL |
| Vanilla extract | 1 tsp. | 5 mL |

Line two 9 x 5 x 3 inch (22 x 12.5 x 7.5 cm) loaf pans with greased foil. Set aside. Stir first 7 ingredients in extra-large bowl until coated with flour. Set aside.

Cream butter and brown sugar in large bowl. Add eggs, 1 at a time, beating well after each addition.

Combine next 4 ingredients in small bowl.

Combine coffee granules and hot water in separate small bowl. Add remaining 3 ingredients. Stir. Add flour mixture to butter mixture in 3 additions, alternating with coffee mixture in 2 additions, stirring well after each addition until just combined. Spread in prepared pans. Bake in 300°F (150°C) oven for about 2 1/2 hours until wooden pick inserted in centre comes out clean. Let stand in pan on wire rack until completely cooled. Makes 2 fruitcakes, about 3 1/4 lbs. (1.5 kg) each. Each cake cuts into 16 slices, for a total of 32 slices.

*1 slice: 332 Calories; 10.8 g Total Fat (4.3 g Mono, 1.5 g Poly, 4.2 g Sat); 39 mg Cholesterol; 59 g Carbohydrate; 3 g Fibre; 4 g Protein; 161 mg Sodium*

Pictured on page 7.

# Dundee Cake

| | | |
|---|---|---|
| Currants | 1 cup | 250 mL |
| Raisins | 1 cup | 250 mL |
| All-purpose flour | 1/3 cup | 75 mL |
| Diced mixed peel | 1/3 cup | 75 mL |
| Red glazed cherries, quartered | 1/3 cup | 75 mL |
| Grated orange zest | 1 tbsp. | 15 mL |
| Butter (or hard margarine), softened | 1 cup | 250 mL |
| Granulated sugar | 1 cup | 250 mL |
| Large eggs | 4 | 4 |
| All-purpose flour | 1 2/3 cups | 400 mL |
| Ground almonds | 2 tbsp. | 30 mL |
| Baking powder | 1 tsp. | 5 mL |
| Corn syrup, warmed | 1 tbsp. | 15 mL |
| Blanched whole almonds, toasted (see Tip, page 96) | 1/2 cup | 125 mL |

*Looking for a fruitcake with a difference? Try this traditional Scottish variation with an attractive topping of whole almonds.*

Line two 8 inch (20 cm) round pans with greased foil. Set aside. Stir first 6 ingredients in medium bowl until coated with flour. Set aside.

Cream butter and sugar in large bowl. Add eggs, 1 at a time, beating well after each addition.

Combine next 3 ingredients in small bowl. Add to butter mixture. Add fruit mixture. Mix well. Spread in prepared pans. Bake in 325°F (160°C) oven for about 1 hour until wooden pick inserted in centre comes out clean. Let stand in pans on wire rack for 5 minutes.

Brush corn syrup over surface of hot cakes (see Note). Arrange almonds in decorative pattern on top. Makes 2 cakes, about 1 1/4 lbs. (560 g) each. Each cake cuts into 8 wedges, for a total of 16 wedges.

*1 wedge: 325 Calories; 15.3 g Total Fat (5.1 g Mono, 1.2 g Poly, 7.8 g Sat); 77 mg Cholesterol; 45 g Carbohydrate; 2 g Fibre; 5 g Protein; 121 mg Sodium*

Pictured on page 7.

**Note:** The corn syrup will be absorbed by the cake, so after it cools the cake won't be sticky.

*All the decadent flavours of an all-time favourite treat—chocolate, pecans and caramel—transformed into a cheesecake.*

Just try to resist a piece of turtle cheesecake when it's decadently decorated with special garnishes! Be as creative as you like, being careful to match the flavours of your garnishes to the flavours of your dessert.

This flashy garnish may be easier to make than you think! First combine 2 cups (500 mL) sugar with 1 cup (250 mL) water in a medium saucepan. Heat and stir on medium-low until the sugar is dissolved. Be sure to brush the side of your saucepan with a wet pastry brush to dissolve any sugar crystals that may form. Boil the mixture on medium-high for 5 to 10 minutes, without stirring, until it becomes a deep, golden-brown colour. Watch carefully to avoid over-cooking. Remove the pan from the heat and drizzle the hot syrup onto a greased baking sheet using a spoon. Be creative and try various shapes and squiggles. Let it stand for about 20 minutes until the sugar hardens before removing your sugary creations from the baking sheet.

# Turtle Cheesecake

| CRUST | | |
|---|---|---|
| Butter (or hard margarine) | 1/2 cup | 125 mL |
| Vanilla wafer crumbs | 2 cups | 500 mL |
| **CARAMEL LAYER** | | |
| Bag of caramels (about 40) | 12 oz. | 340 g |
| Skim evaporated milk | 1/4 cup | 60 mL |
| Chopped pecans, toasted (see Tip, page 96) | 1 cup | 250 mL |
| **CREAM CHEESE LAYER** | | |
| Blocks of light cream cheese (8 oz., 250 g, each), softened | 2 | 2 |
| Granulated sugar | 1/2 cup | 125 mL |
| Vanilla extract | 1 tsp. | 5 mL |
| Large eggs | 2 | 2 |
| Semi-sweet chocolate chips | 1/2 cup | 125 mL |

Whipped cream, for garnish
Chocolate-dipped pecans, for garnish
Sugar shapes, for garnish (see Making Sugar Shapes)
Grated chocolate, for garnish

**Crust:** Melt butter in small saucepan. Remove from heat. Add wafer crumbs. Stir until well mixed. Press firmly into bottom and 1 inch (2.5 cm) up side of ungreased 9 inch (22 cm) springform pan. Bake in 350°F (175°C) oven for 5 minutes. Cool.

**Caramel Layer:** Heat caramels and evaporated milk in medium saucepan on medium-low, stirring often, until smooth. Spread in crust. Sprinkle with pecans.

**Cream Cheese Layer:** Beat first 3 ingredients in large bowl until smooth. Beat in eggs on low, 1 at a time, until just blended.

Heat chocolate chips in small heavy saucepan on lowest heat, stirring constantly, until almost melted. Remove from heat. Stir until smooth. Add to cream cheese mixture. Stir. Pour over pecans. Bake, uncovered, in 350°F (175°C) oven for about 50 minutes until set. Run paring knife around edge of pan to allow cake to settle evenly without cracking. Cool.

*(continued on next page)*

Garnish with whipped cream, chocolate-dipped pecans, sugar shapes and grated chocolate. Cuts into 12 wedges.

*1 wedge:* 460 Calories; 27.6 g Total Fat (8.1 g Mono, 3.1 g Poly, 13.3 g Sat); 78 mg Cholesterol; 47 g Carbohydrate; 2 g Fibre; 8 g Protein; 355 mg Sodium

Pictured on page 3 and below.

*Rich chocolate is paired with the tangy sweetness of orange for a moist and delicious cake. Dress this cake up a bit more by adding some icing.*

# Orange Chocolate Cake

| | | |
|---|---|---|
| Semi-sweet chocolate chips | 1 cup | 250 mL |
| Orange juice | 1/2 cup | 125 mL |
| Butter (or hard margarine), softened | 1 cup | 250 mL |
| Granulated sugar | 2 cups | 500 mL |
| Large eggs | 4 | 4 |
| Vanilla extract | 1 tsp. | 5 mL |
| Orange juice | 1 cup | 250 mL |
| Baking soda | 1 tsp. | 5 mL |
| All-purpose flour | 2 1/2 cups | 625 mL |
| Grated orange zest (see Tip) | 2 tbsp. | 30 mL |
| Salt | 1/2 tsp. | 2 mL |

Combine chocolate chips and first amount of orange juice in small saucepan. Cook, uncovered, on medium for about 5 minutes, stirring often, until chocolate chips are almost melted. Remove from heat. Stir until smooth.

Cream butter and sugar in large bowl. Add eggs, 1 at a time, beating well after each addition. Add vanilla. Beat until fluffy. Add chocolate mixture. Stir.

Stir second amount of orange juice into baking soda in large cup.

Combine remaining 3 ingredients in small bowl. Add flour mixture to butter mixture in 3 additions, alternating with orange juice mixture in 2 additions, stirring well after each addition until just combined. Spread into 3 greased 9 inch (22 cm) round pans. Bake in 350°F (175°C) oven for about 30 minutes until wooden pick inserted in centre comes out clean. Makes 3 cakes. Each cake cuts into 8 wedges, for a total of 24 wedges.

*1 wedge: 224 Calories; 10.5 g Total Fat (3.0 g Mono, 0.5 g Poly, 6.3 g Sat); 51 mg Cholesterol; 31 g Carbohydrate; 1 g Fibre; 3 g Protein; 166 mg Sodium*

*A simple spice cake becomes an elegant holiday treat when it's covered with a white chocolate and orange glaze.*

# Christmas Bundt Cake

| | | |
|---|---|---|
| Large eggs | 3 | 3 |
| Box of spice cake mix (2 layer size) | 1 | 1 |
| Orange juice | 1 1/3 cups | 325 mL |
| Sour cream | 1/3 cup | 75 mL |

*(continued on next page)*

## WHITE CHOCOLATE GLAZE

| | | |
|---|---|---|
| White chocolate chips | 1 cup | 250 mL |
| Whipping cream | 3 tbsp. | 50 mL |
| Grated orange zest (see Tip, page 12) | 2 tsp. | 10 mL |

Beat first 4 ingredients on low in large bowl for about 1 minute until moistened. Beat on medium for 2 minutes. Spread in greased and floured 12 cup (3 L) bundt pan. Bake in 350°F (175°C) oven for 35 to 45 minutes until wooden pick inserted in thickest part of cake comes out clean. Let stand in pan on wire rack for 20 minutes before inverting onto serving plate. Cool completely.

**White Chocolate Glaze:** Heat chocolate chips and whipping cream in small heavy saucepan on lowest heat, stirring often, until chocolate chips are almost melted. Remove from heat. Stir until smooth.

Add orange zest. Stir. Makes about 2/3 cup (150 mL) glaze. Slowly pour over cake, allowing some glaze to run down side. Chill for at least 2 hours until glaze is set. Cuts into 12 wedges.

*1 wedge: 320 Calories; 13.8 g Total Fat (5.6 g Mono, 0.8 g Poly, 6.7 g Sat); 57 mg Cholesterol; 44 g Carbohydrate; 1 Fibre; 6 g Protein; 330 mg Sodium*

Pictured below.

### make ahead

The glazed cake may be stored in an airtight container in the refrigerator for up to 24 hours before serving.

Christmas Bundt Cake, page 12

*This holiday season, please everybody with a classic dessert. Dense, rich dark chocolate cake, paired with whipped cream and sweet cherries.*

# Black Forest Decadence

| | | |
|---|---|---|
| Dark chocolate cake mix (2 layer size) | 1 | 1 |
| Whipping cream | 2 cups | 500 mL |
| Icing (confectioner's) sugar | 1 tbsp. | 15 mL |
| Can of cherry pie filling | 19 oz. | 540 mL |
| **GLAZE** | | |
| Semi-sweet chocolate baking squares (1 oz., 28 g, each), cut up | 6 | 6 |
| Half-and-half cream | 1/2 cup | 125 mL |

Chocolate shavings, for garnish
Cocktail cherries with stems, for garnish

Prepare cake mix according to package directions using 2 greased 9 inch (22 cm) round pans. Cool. Invert onto wire rack. Cut each cake in half horizontally to make 4 layers.

Beat whipping cream and icing sugar in large bowl until stiff peaks form. Transfer 1 cup (250 mL) to small bowl. Chill.

Fold pie filling into remaining whipped cream. Spread about 1 cup (250 mL) cherry mixture over each of 3 layers. Stack. Place remaining layer over top.

**Glaze:** Heat chocolate and cream in medium heavy saucepan on lowest heat, stirring often, until chocolate is almost melted. Remove from heat. Stir until smooth. Set pan in cold water. Whisk until cooled enough to be slightly pourable. Spoon over cake, allowing glaze to run down side. Chill.

Garnish with reserved whipped cream, chocolate shavings and cherries. Cuts into 16 wedges.

*1 wedge: 309 Calories; 19.1 g Total Fat (5.8 g Mono, 3.0 g Poly, 9.2 g Sat); 64 mg Cholesterol; 34 g Carbohydrate; 1 g Fibre; 3 g Protein; 191 mg Sodium*

Pictured at right.

*A traditional Icelandic dessert, perfect for serving at a holiday gathering or buffet. This dense, rich cake is best served in small pieces and must soften for two weeks before serving.*

# Vinarterta

### CAKE LAYERS

| | | |
|---|---|---|
| Butter (or hard margarine), softened | 2 cups | 500 mL |
| Granulated sugar | 1 1/2 cups | 375 mL |
| Large eggs | 2 | 2 |
| Half-and-half cream | 1 tbsp. | 15 mL |
| Almond extract | 1 tsp. | 5 mL |
| All-purpose flour | 4 cups | 1 L |
| Ground almonds | 1/2 cup | 125 mL |
| Baking powder | 2 tsp. | 10 mL |
| Ground cardamom | 1 tsp. | 5 mL |
| Salt, just a pinch | | |

### FILLING

| | | |
|---|---|---|
| Package of pitted prunes | 13 1/4 oz. | 375 g |
| Water | 2 cups | 500 mL |
| Granulated sugar | 1 cup | 250 mL |
| Ground cinnamon | 1 tsp. | 5 mL |
| Vanilla extract | 1 tsp. | 5 mL |

### ALMOND BUTTERCREAM ICING

| | | |
|---|---|---|
| Icing (confectioner's) sugar | 3 3/4 cups | 925 mL |
| Butter, softened | 1 cup | 250 mL |
| Milk | 1/3 cup | 75 mL |
| Almond extract | 3/4 tsp. | 4 mL |

**Cake Layers:** Cream butter and sugar in large bowl until light and creamy. Add eggs, 1 at a time, beating well after each addition. Add cream and almond extract. Beat well.

Combine next 5 ingredients in separate large bowl. Gradually add to butter mixture, stirring until just moistened. Do not overmix. Divide dough into 6 equal portions. Shape each into flattened disc. Wrap each with plastic wrap. Chill for 1 hour. Trace one 8 inch (20 cm) circle on sheet of parchment (not waxed) paper. Turn paper over. Roll out each round to 8 inch (20 cm) circle between 2 sheets of parchment paper on dampened work surface, using sheet with drawing on top as guide. Peel off top sheet of parchment paper to re-use. Place one layer, paper-side down, on ungreased baking sheet. Chill remaining layers. Bake in 350°F (175°C) oven for about 20 minutes until golden brown. Remove layer with paper to wire rack to cool completely. Remove paper. Repeat with remaining layers, baking 1 at a time (see Note).

*(continued on next page)*

**Filling:** Combine prunes and water in large saucepan. Simmer, uncovered, on medium for about 20 minutes, stirring occasionally, until very soft. Drain liquid into small bowl. Set liquid aside.

Add remaining 3 ingredients to prunes in saucepan. Stir until sugar is dissolved. Carefully process in blender or food processor until smooth, adding 1/2 to 3/4 cup (125 to 175 mL) reserved liquid through hole in lid or feed chute until mixture is spreadable and slightly moist (see Safety Tip). Cool completely. Add more liquid to cooled mixture, if necessary, until desired spreading consistency. Place 1 cake layer on separate serving plate. Spread about 1/2 cup (125 mL) filling to edge. Top with second layer. Repeat with remaining filling and cake layers, ending with cake layer on top.

**Almond Buttercream Icing:** Beat all 4 ingredients in large bowl until light and creamy, adding more icing sugar or milk if necessary until spreading consistency. Spread on top and sides of cake. Chill, uncovered, until buttercream is firm. Cover with plastic wrap. Store in refrigerator for 2 weeks before cutting. Cut cake into 3/4 inch (2 cm) wide slices (see diagram). Cut each slice into serving-sized pieces. There will be some irregularly shaped pieces. Makes about 34 pieces.

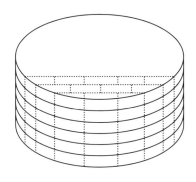

*1 piece: 336 Calories; 17.2 g Total Fat (4.8 g Mono, 0.8 g Poly, 10.4 g Sat); 54 mg Cholesterol; 45 g Carbohydrate; 1 g Fibre; 3 g Protein; 139 mg Sodium*

Pictured below.

**Note:** The layers may break, but after the dessert softens over the 2 week "aging" process, the breaks will not be apparent.

*An upside-down cake may not be traditional holiday fare, but the flavours of pear and gingerbread certainly make this a festive treat.*

# Pear Flower Gingerbread

| Ingredient | Imperial | Metric |
|---|---|---|
| Brown sugar, packed | 1/4 cup | 60 mL |
| Butter (or hard margarine) | 1/4 cup | 60 mL |
| Large peeled pear, core removed, cut into 1/4 inch (6 mm) slices | 1 | 1 |
| Large egg | 1 | 1 |
| Milk | 1/2 cup | 125 mL |
| Fancy (mild) molasses | 1/2 cup | 125 mL |
| Cooking oil | 1/4 cup | 60 mL |
| Whole-wheat flour | 1 1/2 cups | 375 mL |
| Brown sugar, packed | 1/2 cup | 125 mL |
| Ground ginger | 1 tsp. | 5 mL |
| Ground cinnamon | 1 tsp. | 5 mL |
| Ground cloves | 1/2 tsp. | 2 mL |
| Ground nutmeg | 1/2 tsp. | 2 mL |
| Baking soda | 1/2 tsp. | 2 mL |
| Salt | 1/4 tsp. | 1 mL |

Combine first amount of brown sugar and butter in small saucepan on medium. Heat and stir for 3 to 4 minutes until brown sugar is dissolved. Spread evenly in greased 9 inch (22 cm) round pan. Arrange pear slices in flower pattern on top of brown sugar mixture.

Beat egg and milk in large bowl until frothy. Add molasses and cooking oil. Beat until smooth.

Combine remaining 8 ingredients in medium bowl. Add to egg mixture. Stir until just moistened. Carefully pour batter over pear slices. Spread evenly. Bake in 350°F (175°C) oven for about 40 minutes until wooden pick inserted in centre comes out clean. Let stand in pan for 10 minutes. Invert onto serving platter. Cuts into 8 wedges.

*1 wedge: 353 Calories; 13.8 g Total Fat (5.9 g Mono, 2.5 g Poly, 4.5 g Sat); 39 mg Cholesterol; 56 g Carbohydrate; 4 g Fibre; 5 g Protein; 226 mg Sodium*

Pictured on page 21.

# Fig And Pecan Cakes

| | | |
|---|---|---|
| Coarsely chopped dried figs | 1 cup | 250 mL |
| Water | 1 cup | 250 mL |
| Dark raisins | 1/2 cup | 125 mL |
| Baking soda | 1 tsp. | 5 mL |
| Butter (or hard margarine), softened | 1/3 cup | 75 mL |
| Brown sugar, packed | 2/3 cup | 150 mL |
| Large eggs | 2 | 2 |
| Vanilla extract | 1 tsp. | 5 mL |
| Grated orange zest | 2 tsp. | 10 mL |
| All-purpose flour | 1 1/2 cups | 375 mL |
| Coarsely chopped pecans, toasted (see Tip, page 96) | 1 cup | 250 mL |
| Baking powder | 2 tsp. | 10 mL |

*Moist, tender and mildly sweet little cakes are a lovely alternative to the traditional fruitcake. For a special homemade gift, wrap the cakes individually in cellophane and tie with a pretty ribbon.*

Grease six 1 cup (250 mL) ramekins with cooking spray. Line bottom of each with waxed paper. Place ramekins on baking sheet. Set aside. Combine first 4 ingredients in medium saucepan on high. Bring to a boil. Immediately remove from heat. Let stand, uncovered, for about 45 minutes until cool.

Cream butter and brown sugar in large bowl. Add eggs, 1 at a time, beating well after each addition. Add vanilla. Beat until smooth.

Add fig mixture and orange zest. Mix well.

Combine remaining 3 ingredients in small bowl. Add to fig mixture. Mix until no dry flour remains. Spread in prepared ramekins. Bake in 350°F (175°C) oven for about 30 minutes until golden and firm. Let stand in ramekins for 10 minutes before inverting onto wire racks. Discard waxed paper. Cool. Each cake cuts into 4 pieces, for a total of 24 pieces.

*1 piece: 142 Calories; 6.6 g Total Fat (2.8 g Mono, 1.3 g Poly, 2.0 g Sat); 22 mg Cholesterol; 20 g Carbohydrate; 2 g Fibre; 2 g Protein; 101 mg Sodium*

Pictured on page 21.

*This moist, spicy cake is topped with a decadent caramel icing for a deceptively simple, yet utterly delicious dessert.*

## christmas fun

As the story goes, author William Sydney Porter (who used the pen name O. Henry) was notorious for missing deadlines, including the one for a Christmas story he was hired to write in 1906. When the artist who was to illustrate Porter's story asked what he should be drawing, Porter confessed that he hadn't written a word, but had a vague image of a long-haired woman and a man holding a watch in a poorly furnished room. As the artist drew, Porter penned the tale of an impoverished wife who sells her beautiful hair to buy a watch fob for her husband, unaware that he has sold his watch to buy hair combs for her. *The Gift of the Magi* would go on to become a holiday classic.

# Boiled Raisin Cake

| | | |
|---|---|---|
| Water | 2 cups | 500 mL |
| Raisins | 1 1/2 cups | 375 mL |
| All-purpose flour | 1 3/4 cups | 425 mL |
| Baking powder | 1 1/2 tsp. | 7 mL |
| Ground cinnamon | 3/4 tsp. | 4 mL |
| Baking soda | 1/2 tsp. | 2 mL |
| Ground nutmeg | 1/2 tsp. | 2 mL |
| Salt | 1/2 tsp. | 2 mL |
| Large egg, fork-beaten | 1 | 1 |
| Brown sugar, packed | 1 cup | 250 mL |
| Butter (or hard margarine), softened | 1/2 cup | 125 mL |
| Vanilla extract | 1 tsp. | 5 mL |
| **CARAMEL ICING** | | |
| Brown sugar, packed | 1/2 cup | 125 mL |
| Butter (or hard margarine) | 1/4 cup | 60 mL |
| Milk | 3 tbsp. | 50 mL |
| Icing (confectioner's) sugar | 1 1/2 cups | 375 mL |

Combine water and raisins in small saucepan. Bring to a boil. Boil gently, uncovered, for 6 minutes. Drain, reserving 2/3 cup (150 mL) liquid in small cup.

Combine next 6 ingredients in medium bowl.

Beat next 4 ingredients in large bowl until combined. Add flour mixture to butter mixture in 3 additions, alternating with raisins and reserved liquid in 2 additions, stirring well after each addition until just combined. Transfer to greased 9 x 9 inch (22 x 22 cm) pan. Bake in 350°F (175°C) oven for about 40 minutes until wooden pick inserted in centre comes out clean.

**Caramel Icing:** Combine first 3 ingredients in small saucepan. Heat and stir until boiling. Boil, uncovered, for 2 minutes. Remove from heat. Cool.

Add icing sugar. Beat until smooth spreading consistency. Makes about 3/4 cup (175 mL) icing. Spread over cake. Cuts into 12 pieces.

*1 piece: 393 Calories; 12.0 g Total Fat (3.2 g Mono, 0.5 g Poly, 7.4 g Sat); 46 mg Cholesterol; 72 g Carbohydrate; 2 g Fibre; 3 g Protein; 284 mg Sodium*

Pictured at right.

1. Pear Flower Gingerbread, page 18
2. Fig And Pecan Cakes, page 19
3. Boiled Raisin Cake, page 20

*If chocolate truffles are your favourite sweet, indulge in a wedge of this decadent, dark chocolate-filled dessert.*

## food fun

Ever had one of those chocolate cravings that just won't subside until you've indulged? Noticed how sometimes a piece of chocolate just makes things seem a little better? There's more to this super-soother than its sweet, creamy taste. Chocolate contains low levels of chemicals that create feelings of happiness—some experts even suggest these feelings mimic those felt when a person falls in love. That just might explain why most people love chocolate!

# Chocolate Truffle

### CHOCOLATE CRUST

| | | |
|---|---|---|
| Butter (or hard margarine) | 1/4 cup | 60 mL |
| Chocolate wafer crumbs | 1 1/4 cups | 300 mL |
| Granulated sugar | 1 tbsp. | 15 mL |

### CHOCOLATE FILLING

| | | |
|---|---|---|
| Butter (or hard margarine) | 1 cup | 250 mL |
| Semi-sweet chocolate chips | 3 cups | 750 mL |
| Large eggs, room temperature | 5 | 5 |
| Vanilla extract | 1 tsp. | 5 mL |

### CHOCOLATE GLAZE

| | | |
|---|---|---|
| Semi-sweet chocolate chips | 1/2 cup | 125 mL |
| Evaporated milk (or whipping cream) | 3 tbsp. | 50 mL |

### TOPPING

| | | |
|---|---|---|
| Whipping cream | 1 cup | 250 mL |
| Granulated sugar | 2 tsp. | 10 mL |
| Vanilla extract | 1/2 tsp. | 2 mL |

Grated chocolate, for garnish

**Chocolate Crust:** Melt butter in medium saucepan. Remove from heat. Stir in wafer crumbs and sugar. Press firmly in bottom of ungreased 8 inch (20 cm) springform pan. Set pan on piece of foil. Press foil up all around to prevent water leaking into pan. Set pan in roaster or other wide pan.

**Chocolate Filling:** Melt butter in large heavy saucepan on lowest heat. Add chocolate chips. Heat and stir until almost melted. Remove from heat. Stir until smooth. Transfer to medium bowl.

Add eggs, 1 at a time, beating well after each addition. Add vanilla. Stir. Pour over crust in pan. Carefully pour boiling water into roasting pan until halfway up side of springform pan. Bake in 425°F (220°C) oven for about 15 minutes until outer edge is set. Centre will still be soft but will set upon cooling. Remove springform pan to wire rack. Cool. Chill for at least 4 hours. Remove sides of springform pan.

*(continued on next page)*

**Chocolate Glaze:** Combine chocolate chips and evaporated milk in small saucepan on low. Heat and stir until smooth. Pour over filling. Spread over top and sides. Let stand for 5 minutes before adding topping.

**Topping:** Beat first 3 ingredients in small bowl until stiff peaks form. Drop by rounded spoonfuls around edge of cake.

Sprinkle with grated chocolate. Chill until ready to serve. Cuts into 12 wedges.

*1 wedge:* 559 Calories; 44.4 g Total Fat (13.3 g Mono, 2.2 g Poly, 26.2 g Sat); 154 mg Cholesterol; 42 g Carbohydrate; 3 g Fibre; 6 g Protein; 244 mg Sodium

Pictured below.

*Add a tropical twist to your holidays with this golden, rum-flavoured pound cake.*

# Rum Cake

| | | |
|---|---|---|
| Butter (or hard margarine), softened | 1 cup | 250 mL |
| Granulated sugar | 1 3/4 cups | 425 mL |
| Large eggs | 4 | 4 |
| Rum extract | 1 tsp. | 5 mL |
| All-purpose flour | 3 cups | 750 mL |
| Baking powder | 1/2 tsp. | 2 mL |
| Baking soda | 1/2 tsp. | 2 mL |
| Salt | 1/2 tsp. | 2 mL |
| Buttermilk | 1 cup | 250 mL |

Cream butter and sugar in large bowl. Add eggs, 1 at a time, beating well after each addition. Add extract. Stir.

Combine next 4 ingredients in medium bowl.

Add flour mixture to butter mixture in 3 additions, alternating with buttermilk in 2 additions, stirring well after each addition until just combined. Transfer to greased 10 inch (25 cm) angel food tube pan. Bake in 325°F (160°C) oven for about 1 1/4 hours until wooden pick inserted in centre comes out clean. Cuts into 12 wedges.

*1 wedge: 376 Calories; 17.0 g Total Fat (4.7 g Mono, 0.8 g Poly, 10.2 g Sat); 103 mg Cholesterol; 51 g Carbohydrate; 1 g Fibre; 6 g Protein; 311 mg Sodium*

*This rustic-looking dessert is a breeze to put together with the help of a few simple, convenient ingredients. Serve warm with vanilla ice cream or cold with whipped cream.*

# Cherry Strudel Dessert

| | | |
|---|---|---|
| Package of puff pastry, thawed according to package directions | 14 oz. | 397 g |
| Vanilla wafer crumbs | 1/4 cup | 60 mL |
| Can of cherry pie filling | 19 oz. | 540 mL |
| Grated lemon zest | 2 tsp. | 10 mL |
| Vanilla wafer crumbs | 2 tbsp. | 30 mL |
| Sliced almonds | 1/4 cup | 60 mL |

*(continued on next page)*

Roll out puff pastry on lightly floured surface to 12 x 16 inch (30 x 40 cm) rectangle. Transfer to greased baking sheet.

Sprinkle first amount of wafer crumbs over pastry to within 1 inch (2.5 cm) of edge.

Combine pie filling and lemon zest in medium bowl. Spoon over wafer crumbs. Carefully spread to within 2 inches (5 cm) of edge of pastry. Fold section of border up and over edge of filling. Repeat with next section, allowing pastry to overlap so that fold is created. Pinch to seal. Repeat until pastry border is completely folded around filling.

Sprinkle second amount of wafer crumbs and almonds over exposed cherry filling. Bake on bottom rack in 400°F (205°C) oven for about 30 minutes until golden. Let stand for 10 minutes before cutting. Serves 8.

*1 serving: 393 Calories; 21.8 g Total Fat (12.4 g Mono, 3.1 g Poly, 5.1 g Sat); 2 mg Cholesterol; 45 g Carbohydrate; 2 g Fibre; 5 g Protein; 149 mg Sodium*

Pictured below.

Cherry Strudel Dessert, page 24

*Summer may be long gone, but you can still enjoy those summery flavours in a dessert made with canned and frozen fruit. Mellow pear and tangy raspberries are a perfect combination.*

# Fruit Cobbler

| | | |
|---|---|---|
| Can of pear halves in light syrup, drained and syrup reserved, cut up | 14 oz. | 398 mL |
| Container of frozen raspberries in syrup, thawed, drained and syrup reserved | 15 oz. | 425 g |
| Granulated sugar | 1/3 cup | 75 mL |
| All-purpose flour | 1 1/2 tbsp. | 25 mL |
| Ground cinnamon | 1/4 tsp. | 1 mL |
| Reserved raspberry syrup, plus pear syrup to make | 3/4 cup | 175 mL |
| TOPPING | | |
| Large egg | 1 | 1 |
| Butter (or hard margarine), melted | 1/4 cup | 60 mL |
| Milk | 1/3 cup | 75 mL |
| All-purpose flour | 1 cup | 250 mL |
| Granulated sugar | 1/4 cup | 60 mL |
| Baking powder | 1 1/2 tsp. | 7 mL |
| Salt | 1/4 tsp. | 1 mL |

Layer pear and raspberries, in order given, in ungreased 2 quart (2 L) casserole.

Combine next 3 ingredients in small saucepan. Add reserved juices. Mix well. Heat and stir until boiling and thickened. Pour over fruit. Stir. Bake, uncovered, in 425°F (220°C) oven for 10 minutes.

**Topping:** Beat egg in medium bowl. Add butter and milk. Stir.

Sprinkle next 4 ingredients over butter mixture. Stir until just moistened. Spoon mounds of batter, using 1 tbsp. (15 mL) for each, in single layer over fruit mixture. Bake, uncovered, for about 20 minutes until golden and wooden pick inserted in centre of topping comes out clean. Serves 6.

*1 serving: 380 Calories; 8.6 g Total Fat (2.4 g Mono, 0.4 g Poly, 5.1 g Sat); 52 mg Cholesterol; 73 g Carbohydrate; 3 g Fibre; 5 g Protein; 449 mg Sodium*

Pictured at right.

# Brown Betty

| Sliced peeled cooking apple (such as McIntosh) | 6 cups | 1.5 L |
|---|---|---|
| Granulated sugar | 3/4 cup | 175 mL |
| **TOPPING** | | |
| All-purpose flour | 1 1/4 cups | 300 mL |
| Brown sugar, packed | 3/4 cup | 175 mL |
| Butter (or hard margarine) | 1/2 cup | 125 mL |
| Salt | 1/2 tsp. | 2 mL |

Put apple into greased 10 inch (25 cm) round casserole. Sprinkle with granulated sugar.

**Topping:** Mix first 4 ingredients in small bowl until mixture resembles coarse crumbs. Scatter over apples. Pat down lightly. Bake, uncovered, in 375°F (190°C) oven for about 40 minutes until topping is golden and apples are tender. Serves 8.

*1 serving: 350 Calories; 11.5 g Total Fat (3.0 g Mono, 0.5 g Poly, 7.2 g Sat); 30 mg Cholesterol; 62 g Carbohydrate; 1 g Fibre; 2 g Protein; 235 mg Sodium*

Pictured below.

*This simple dessert has been around since colonial America—and just one bite will tell you why! Great served hot or cold, and always with cream or ice cream.*

Left: Fruit Cobbler, page 26
Right: Brown Betty, above

*Packed with tender, juicy raisins, this warming dessert is sure to provide a festive change from the standard apple or berry fillings.*

## variation

Not keen on raisins? Use your favourite flavour of pie filling instead.

# Raisin Cobbler

| Can of raisin pie filling | 19 oz. | 540 mL |
|---|---|---|
| Lemon juice | 1 tsp. | 5 mL |
| **TOPPING** | | |
| Large egg, fork-beaten | 1 | 1 |
| Cooking oil | 1/3 cup | 75 mL |
| Milk | 1/3 cup | 75 mL |
| All-purpose flour | 1 1/2 cups | 375 mL |
| Granulated sugar | 1/3 cup | 75 mL |
| Baking powder | 2 tsp. | 10 mL |
| Salt | 1/2 tsp. | 2 mL |

Combine pie filling and lemon juice in ungreased 8 inch (20 cm) round casserole. Spread evenly. Bake in 400°F (205°C) oven for 10 minutes.

**Topping:** Combine first 3 ingredients in medium bowl.

Sprinkle remaining 4 ingredients over milk mixture. Stir until just moistened. Remove casserole from oven. Spoon mounds of batter, using 1 tbsp. (15 mL) for each, in single layer over pie filling. Bake, uncovered, for another 20 to 25 minutes until wooden pick inserted in centre of topping comes out clean. Remove to wire rack. Let stand for 5 minutes. Serve warm. Serves 6.

*1 serving: 372 Calories; 13.1 g Total Fat (7.6 g Mono, 3.7 g Poly, 1.2 g Sat); 32 mg Cholesterol; 59 g Carbohydrate; 1 g Fibre; 5 g Protein; 315 mg Sodium*

Pictured at right.

*Comfort food is part of what makes the holidays special. This family favourite is improved with the addition of caramel and a hint of tangy lemon. Perfect for a cold, wintry evening.*

# Caramel Apple Crisp

| Sliced peeled cooking apple (such as McIntosh) | 4 1/2 cups | 1.1 L |
|---|---|---|
| Brown sugar, packed | 1/2 cup | 125 mL |
| Water | 1/4 cup | 60 mL |
| Caramels | 16 | 16 |
| Lemon juice | 1 tbsp. | 15 mL |

*(continued on next page)*

## TOPPING

| | | |
|---|---|---|
| All-purpose flour | 1/3 cup | 75 mL |
| Granulated sugar | 1/4 cup | 60 mL |
| Butter (or hard margarine), softened | 2 tbsp. | 30 mL |
| Ground cinnamon | 1/4 tsp. | 1 mL |

Combine first 3 ingredients in large saucepan on medium. Cook, covered, for about 15 minutes, stirring occasionally, until apple is tender-crisp. Transfer apple to medium bowl using slotted spoon.

Add caramels and lemon juice to apple liquid. Heat and stir until caramels are melted and smooth. Add apple. Stir. Transfer to greased 2 quart (2 L) casserole.

**Topping:** Mix all 4 ingredients in small bowl until mixture resembles coarse crumbs. Sprinkle over apple mixture. Bake, uncovered, in 375°F (190°C) oven for about 35 minutes until top is golden and bubbling. Serves 8.

*1 serving: 208 Calories; 4.2 g Total Fat (0.9 g Mono, 0.2 g Poly, 2.9 g Sat); 9 mg Cholesterol; 44 g Carbohydrate; 1 g Fibre; 1 g Protein; 65 mg Sodium*

Pictured below.

Left: Raisin Cobbler, page 28
Right: Caramel Apple Crisp, page 28

## food fun

From Hansel and Gretel's cottage to the run-away cookie of fairy-tale fame, there's something a little bit magical about gingerbread, which might help explain why it's associated with the most magical time of the year. This spicy cookie has been a festive favourite since the Middle Ages. Why not whip up a batch today and bring a little of that holiday magic to your own kitchen?

# Gingerbread Stars

| | | |
|---|---|---|
| Butter (or hard margarine), softened | 1/2 cup | 125 mL |
| Brown sugar, packed | 1/2 cup | 125 mL |
| Ground ginger | 1 1/4 tsp. | 6 mL |
| Baking powder | 1 tsp. | 5 mL |
| Ground cinnamon | 3/4 tsp. | 4 mL |
| Baking soda | 1/2 tsp. | 2 mL |
| Salt | 1/4 tsp. | 1 mL |
| Ground cloves | 1/8 tsp. | 0.5 mL |
| Large egg | 1 | 1 |
| Fancy (mild) molasses | 1/2 cup | 125 mL |
| White vinegar | 1 tbsp. | 15 mL |
| All-purpose flour | 2 1/2 cups | 625 mL |
| HONEY LEMON ICING | | |
| Liquid honey | 2 tbsp. | 30 mL |
| Lemon juice | 2 tbsp. | 30 mL |
| Icing (confectioner's) sugar | 2 1/2 cups | 625 mL |
| Gold or silver dragées (see Note), optional | | |

Beat butter in large bowl for 1 minute. Add next 7 ingredients. Beat well.

Add next 3 ingredients. Beat until smooth. Mixture will look slightly curdled.

Add half of flour. Beat well. Add remaining flour. Mix well. Divide dough in half. Wrap each half in plastic wrap. Chill for at least 3 hours. Roll out 1 portion of dough on lightly floured surface to 1/4 inch (6 mm) thickness. Cut out shapes with lightly floured 2 1/2 inch (6.4 cm) star cookie cutter. Roll out scraps to cut more stars. Repeat with remaining portion of dough. Arrange cookies, about 1 inch (2.5 cm) apart, on greased cookie sheets. Bake in 375°F (190°C) oven for about 8 minutes until edges start to brown. Let stand on cookie sheets for 5 minutes. Remove cookies from cookie sheets and place on wire racks to cool completely.

**Honey Lemon Icing:** Combine honey and lemon juice in medium heatproof bowl or top of double boiler. Place over small saucepan of simmering water. Heat and stir for about 4 minutes, adding icing sugar, 1 tbsp. (15 mL) at a time, until barely pourable consistency. Makes about 2/3 cup (150 mL) icing. Spoon into piping bag fitted with small plain writing tip or small resealable freezer bag with tiny piece snipped off corner.

*(continued on next page)*

Decorate cookies with icing and dragées. Work quickly, as icing sets almost immediately. Makes about 42 cookies.

*1 cookie: 91 Calories; 2.3 g Total Fat (0.6 g Mono, 0.1 g Poly, 1.4 g Sat); 10 mg Cholesterol; 17 g Carbohydrate; trace Fibre; 1 g Protein; 55 mg Sodium*

Pictured on front cover, page 3 and below.

**Note:** Dragées (pronounced dra-ZHAYS) are tiny round, hard candies used for decorating. They are usually silver or gold-coloured.

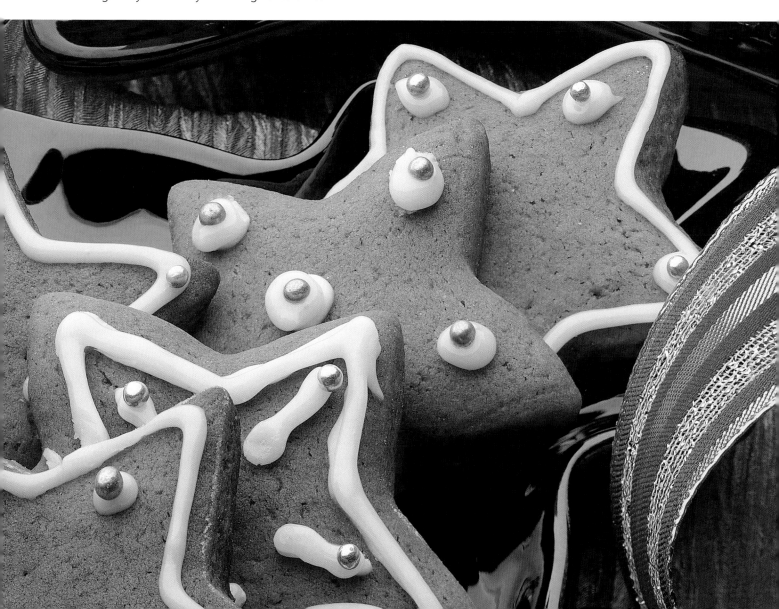

*For a truly authentic shortbread, the secret ingredient is real butter—margarine just can't compare! Making the dough in your food processor is a real time-saver!*

# Shortbread

| All-purpose flour | 1 3/4 cups | 425 mL |
| Butter, softened and cut up | 1 cup | 250 mL |
| Icing (confectioner's) sugar | 1/3 cup | 75 mL |
| Cornstarch | 1/4 cup | 60 mL |
| Vanilla extract | 1/2 tsp. | 2 mL |
| Salt, just a pinch | | |

Process all 6 ingredients in food processor for about 10 seconds until ball forms. Transfer to work surface. Roll dough into two 1 1/4 inch (3 cm) diameter logs. Wrap tightly in waxed paper. Chill for at least 1 hour or overnight. Discard wax paper. Cut into 1/4 inch (6 mm) slices. Arrange on 2 ungreased cookie sheets. Bake on separate racks in 325°F (160°C) oven for about 15 minutes, switching position of pans at halftime, until golden on bottom and sides. Remove cookies from cookie sheets and place on wire rack to cool. Makes about 48 cookies.

*1 shortbread: 54 Calories; 3.8 g Total Fat (1.0 g Mono, 0.1 g Poly, 2.4 g Sat); 10 mg Cholesterol; 5 g Carbohydrate; trace Fibre; trace Protein; 27 mg Sodium*

Pictured at right and on back cover.

*A perfect twist on tradition—brown sugar creates a butterscotch flavour in this rich shortbread. Perfect for serving with tea.*

## about shortbread

Shortbread was once associated primarily with Christmas and Hogmanay, or Scottish New Year's Eve, but this classic cookie is now considered a year-round favourite. Rich and buttery, shortbread was traditionally made by pressing the dough into a decorative round mold. After baking, the large cookie was then cut into wedges.

# Butterscotch Shortbread

| Butter, softened | 1 cup | 250 mL |
| Brown sugar, packed | 2/3 cup | 150 mL |
| | | |
| All-purpose flour | 2 cups | 500 mL |
| Graham cracker crumbs | 1/2 cup | 125 mL |

Cream butter and brown sugar in medium bowl.

Combine flour and graham crumbs in small bowl. Add to butter mixture. Mix until soft, slightly crumbly dough forms. Turn out onto lightly floured surface. Knead for about 2 minutes until smooth. Press into ungreased 8 x 8 inch (20 x 20 cm) pan. Prick top of dough in several places with a fork. Score dough into 12 rectangles with sharp knife. Score rectangles diagonally into 24 triangles. Bake in 300°F (150°C) oven for about 30 minutes until edges are golden. Let stand in pan on wire rack until cooled completely. Cut along scoring into triangles. Makes 24 triangles.

*1 triangle: 131 Calories; 7.8 g Total Fat (2.0 g Mono, 0.4 g Poly, 4.8 g Sat); 20 mg Cholesterol; 15 g Carbohydrate; trace Fibre; 1 g Protein; 67 mg Sodium*

Pictured at right and on back cover.

Left: Butterscotch Shortbread, page 32
Right: Shortbread, page 32

*A tiny dab of mincemeat adds festive flair to pecan-coated thimble cookies. A hint of cinnamon and nutmeg provides the perfect finishing touch.*

# Mincemeat Bites

| | | |
|---|---|---|
| Butter (or hard margarine), softened | 1/2 cup | 125 mL |
| Granulated sugar | 1/2 cup | 125 mL |
| Egg yolk (large) | 1 | 1 |
| Rum extract | 1 tsp. | 5 mL |
| All-purpose flour | 1 1/4 cups | 300 mL |
| Baking powder | 1/4 tsp. | 1 mL |
| Salt | 1/4 tsp. | 1 mL |
| Ground pecans | 2/3 cup | 150 mL |
| Granulated sugar | 3 tbsp. | 50 mL |
| Egg white (large) | 1 | 1 |
| Ground cinnamon | 1/8 tsp. | 0.5 mL |
| Ground nutmeg, sprinkle | | |
| Mincemeat | 3 tbsp. | 50 mL |

Cream butter and first amount of sugar in medium bowl. Add egg yolk and extract. Beat until smooth.

Combine next 3 ingredients in small bowl. Stir. Add to butter mixture. Stir until combined. Roll into 1 inch (2.5 cm) balls.

Combine pecans and second amount of sugar in small shallow dish.

Beat next 3 ingredients with fork in separate small bowl. Dip 1 ball into egg white mixture. Roll in pecan mixture until coated. Repeat with remaining balls, egg white mixture and pecan mixture. Arrange, about 2 inches (5 cm) apart, on well-greased cookie sheets. Dent each ball with thumb.

Spoon about 1/4 tsp. (1 mL) mincemeat into each dent. Bake in 325°F (160°C) oven for 18 to 20 minutes until edges are golden. Let stand on cookie sheets for 5 minutes. Remove cookies from cookie sheets and place on wire racks to cool. Makes about 36 cookies.

*1 cookie: 71 Calories; 4.3 g Total Fat (1.6 g Mono, 0.6 g Poly, 1.8 g Sat); 12 mg Cholesterol; 8 g Carbohydrate; trace Fibre; 1 g Protein; 38 mg Sodium*

Pictured on page 37.

# Fruit Scrolls

| | | |
|---|---|---|
| Butter (or hard margarine), softened | 1 cup | 250 mL |
| Brown sugar, packed | 2 cups | 500 mL |
| Large eggs | 3 | 3 |
| All-purpose flour | 4 1/2 cups | 1.1 L |
| Ground cinnamon | 1/2 tsp. | 2 mL |
| Ground ginger | 1/2 tsp. | 2 mL |
| Ground cloves | 1/4 tsp. | 1 mL |
| Mincemeat with rum and brandy, processed until slightly smooth | 2 cups | 500 mL |

*Add elegance to your holiday cookie tray with these pretty palmier-style cookies. Attractive swirls of mincemeat filling make for an unforgettable presentation.*

Cream butter and brown sugar in extra-large bowl until light and creamy. Add eggs, 1 at a time, beating well after each addition.

Combine next 4 ingredients in large bowl. Add to sugar mixture in 3 batches, mixing well after each addition, until no dry flour remains. Turn out onto lightly floured work surface. Shape mixture into ball. Divide into 4 equal portions. Shape each portion into flattened square. Wrap each square with plastic wrap. Chill for 3 hours.

Roll out each square between 2 sheets of waxed paper on dampened work surface to 10 x 14 inch (25 x 35 cm) rectangle, about 1/4 inch (6 mm) thick. Remove and discard top sheet of waxed paper from each square. Spread 1 rectangle with 1/2 cup (125 mL) mincemeat to edges. Roll up halfway, jelly roll-style, from long side using bottom piece of waxed paper as guide. Repeat from opposite long side until rolls meet in centre. Discard waxed paper. Place scroll on ungreased cookie sheet. Repeat with remaining squares and mincemeat, for a total of 4 rolls. Cover. Freeze for about 2 hours until firm. Cut each roll into 1/2 inch (12 mm) thick slices. Arrange, cut-side down, on greased cookie sheets. Bake in 350°F (175°C) oven for 10 to 15 minutes until golden brown and firm. Let stand on cookie sheets for 5 minutes. Remove cookies from cookie sheets and place on wire racks to cool. Cool cookie sheets between batches. Makes about 108 cookies.

*1 cookie: 59 Calories; 2.1 g Total Fat (0.6 g Mono, 0.1 g Poly, 1.3 g Sat); 10 mg Cholesterol; 10 g Carbohydrate; trace Fibre; 1 g Protein; 16 mg Sodium*

Pictured on page 37.

*Replace pie crust with puff pastry for a whole new take on the classic mincemeat pie. A sprinkle of sanding sugar adds sparkle and crunch.*

### about mincemeat

How did something made of fruit and spices get the name "mincemeat?" There may not be meat in the mix now—but there used to be. The first mincemeat pies were meat pies with fruit and brandy or wine added as preservatives. Over the years, this savoury main course got sweeter and evolved into a dessert, though many people still enjoy the savoury version of mincemeat made with exactly that—minced meat.

# Mincemeat Puffs

| | | |
|---|---|---|
| Package of puff pastry, thawed according to package directions | 14 oz. | 397 g |
| Large egg | 1 | 1 |
| Milk | 1 tsp. | 5 mL |
| Mincemeat with rum and brandy, packed | 3/4 cup | 175 mL |
| Sanding (decorating) sugar (see Tip, page 84) | 4 tsp. | 20 mL |

Roll out half of pastry on lightly floured surface to 9 x 9 inch (22 x 22 cm) square. Cut into nine 3 inch (7.5 cm) squares. Repeat with remaining pastry, for a total of 18 squares.

Beat egg and milk with fork in small bowl.

Place 2 tsp. (10 mL) mincemeat in centre of each pastry square. Brush edges with egg mixture. Fold in half over filling. Pinch edges to seal, pressing out any air bubbles. Arrange pastries, about 2 inches (5 cm) apart, on greased cookie sheets. Pierce each pastry several times with knife. Brush tops with remaining egg mixture.

Sprinkle sanding sugar over each pastry. Bake in 400°F (205°C) oven for about 15 minutes until golden. Makes 18 puffs.

*1 puff: 152 Calories; 9.3 g Total Fat (5.1 g Mono, 1.2 g Poly, 2.6 g Sat); 11 mg Cholesterol; 15 g Carbohydrate; 1 g Fibre; 2 g Protein; 60 mg Sodium*

Pictured at right.

1. Mincemeat Puffs, above
2. Mincemeat Bites, page 34
3. Fruit Scrolls, page 35

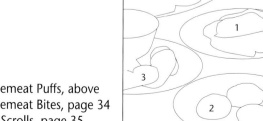

*This versatile dough is the starting point for all sorts of cookie creations! Cut out your favourite shapes and decorate with a bright-coloured glaze or sprinkles.*

# Basic Sugar Cookies

| | | |
|---|---|---|
| Butter (or hard margarine), softened | 1 cup | 250 mL |
| Granulated sugar | 1 cup | 250 mL |
| Egg yolks (large) | 2 | 2 |
| Vanilla extract | 1/2 tsp. | 2 mL |
| All-purpose flour | 2 1/2 cups | 625 mL |
| Baking powder | 1/2 tsp. | 2 mL |
| Salt | 1/2 tsp. | 2 mL |
| **BASIC COOKIE GLAZE** | | |
| Icing (confectioner's) sugar | 3/4 cup | 175 mL |
| Milk | 1 tbsp. | 15 mL |
| Butter (or hard margarine), softened | 2 tsp. | 10 mL |
| Vanilla extract | 1/4 tsp. | 1 mL |
| Liquid (or paste) food colouring (see Tip) | | |

Cream butter and granulated sugar in large bowl. Add egg yolks 1 at a time, beating well after each addition. Add vanilla. Beat until smooth.

Combine next 3 ingredients in small bowl. Add to butter mixture in 2 additions, mixing well after each addition until no dry flour remains. Divide dough in half. Shape each half into slightly flattened disc. Wrap with plastic wrap. Chill for 1 hour. Discard plastic wrap from 1 disc. Roll out dough between 2 sheets of waxed paper to about 1/8 inch (3 mm) thickness. Discard top sheet of waxed paper. Cut out shapes with lightly floured cookie cutters. Roll out scraps to cut more shapes. Arrange, about 1 inch (2.5 cm) apart, on greased cookie sheets. Bake in 350°F (175°C) oven for 6 to 8 minutes until edges are golden. Let stand on cookie sheets for 5 minutes. Remove cookies from cookie sheets and place on wire racks to cool completely. Cool cookie sheets between batches. Repeat with remaining disc.

**Basic Cookie Glaze:** Beat first 4 ingredients in small bowl, adding more icing sugar or milk if necessary, until barely pourable consistency.

Add food colouring 1 drop at a time, stirring well after each addition, until desired colour is reached. Makes about 3/4 cup (175 mL) glaze. Spoon into small resealable plastic bag with tiny piece snipped off corner. Drizzle glaze over each cookie. Makes about 36 cookies.

*1 cookie: 108 Calories; 5.5 g Total Fat (1.5 g Mono, 0.2 g Poly, 3.4 g Sat); 24 mg Cholesterol; 14 g Carbohydrate; trace Fibre; 1 g Protein; 74 mg Sodium*

Pictured at right.

*The holidays are the perfect time for fancy treats. These cookies look impressive, but are simple enough for kids to make.*

# Swirling Dervish Cookies

| | | |
|---|---|---|
| Chocolate hazelnut spread | 1/2 cup | 125 mL |
| Chopped walnuts | 1/3 cup | 75 mL |
| All-purpose flour | 1 1/4 cups | 300 mL |
| Baking powder | 1/4 tsp. | 1 mL |
| Salt | 1/4 tsp. | 1 mL |
| Butter (or hard margarine), softened | 1/2 cup | 125 mL |
| Granulated sugar | 1/2 cup | 125 mL |
| Egg yolk (large) | 1 | 1 |
| Vanilla extract | 1/4 tsp. | 1 mL |

Combine chocolate spread and walnuts in small bowl.

Combine next 3 ingredients in separate small bowl.

Cream butter and sugar in large bowl. Add egg yolk and vanilla. Beat until smooth. Add flour mixture. Stir to combine. Shape dough into ball. Roll out dough between 2 sheets of waxed paper to 8 x 10 inch (20 x 25 cm) rectangle. Discard top sheet of waxed paper. Spread chocolate mixture over dough, leaving 1/2 inch (12 mm) border at each long edge. Roll up tightly from long side, jelly roll-style, using waxed paper as a guide. Press seam against roll to seal. Wrap with plastic wrap. Chill for about 1 hour until firm. Discard plastic wrap. Cut with serrated knife into 1/4 inch (6 mm) slices. Arrange slices, about 1 inch (2.5 cm) apart, on greased cookie sheets. Bake in 350°F (175°C) oven for 10 to 12 minutes until golden. Let stand on cookie sheets for 5 minutes. Remove cookies from cookie sheets and place on wire racks to cool. Cool cookie sheets between batches. Makes about 36 cookies.

*1 cookie: 70 Calories; 4.1 g Total Fat (1.3 g Mono, 0.7 g Poly, 1.9 g Sat); 12 mg Cholesterol; 8 g Carbohydrate; trace Fibre; 1 g Protein; 37 mg Sodium*

Pictured on page 43.

# Chocolate Sandwiches

| | | |
|---|---|---|
| Semi-sweet chocolate square (1 oz., 28 g) | 1 | 1 |
| Butter (or hard margarine), softened | 1/2 cup | 125 mL |
| Granulated sugar | 1/4 cup | 60 mL |
| All-purpose flour | 1 cup | 250 mL |
| ICING | | |
| Butter (or hard margarine), softened | 2 tbsp. | 30 mL |
| Icing (confectioner's) sugar | 1/3 cup | 75 mL |
| Semi-sweet chocolate chips, melted | 1/3 cup | 75 mL |
| Semi-sweet chocolate squares (1 oz., 28 g, each) | 7 | 7 |

Heat chocolate in small heavy saucepan on lowest heat, stirring often, until chocolate is almost melted. Remove from heat. Stir until smooth.

Cream first amount of butter and granulated sugar in medium bowl. Add melted chocolate. Stir. Add flour. Mix well. Cover. Chill overnight. Roll out on lightly floured surface to 8 x 14 inch (20 x 35 cm) rectangle. Cut into 2 x 2 inch (5 x 5 cm) squares. Transfer to greased cookie sheets. Bake in 350°F (175°C) oven for about 10 minutes until crisp. Let stand on cookie sheets for 5 minutes. Remove cookies from cookie sheets and place on wire racks to cool completely. Makes 28 cookies.

**Icing:** Beat first 3 ingredients in small bowl until smooth. Spread on 14 cookies. Press remaining 14 cookies over icing to make sandwiches. Place 4 sandwiches on wire rack set over large plate.

Heat chocolate in small heavy saucepan on lowest heat, stirring often, until chocolate is almost melted. Remove from heat. Stir until smooth. Spoon melted chocolate over sandwiches, allowing chocolate to cover tops and sides. Transfer to waxed paper to set. Repeat with remaining sandwiches. Return chocolate on plate to saucepan and reheat to coat more sandwiches. Makes 14 chocolate sandwiches.

*1 sandwich: 213 Calories; 11.8 g Total Fat (3.3 g Mono, 0.5 g Poly, 7.2 g Sat); 22 mg Cholesterol; 28 g Carbohydrate; 1 g Fibre; 2 g Protein; 59 mg Sodium*

Pictured on page 43.

*Some sandwiches use bread to hold their fillings, but the best ones use cookies instead! These sweet sandwiches use crisp chocolate cookies to hold a delicious filling of chocolate icing.*

### christmas fun

Christmas parades have long been a tradition, starting just about the same time Christmas was first celebrated! This tradition has changed greatly over time, thus resulting in the massive commercial pageants of today. Interestingly, the first Santa Claus parade, a long-time North American custom, was held in Toronto in 1905 and boasted only a single float!

*You'll never complain about fingerprints again, at least not when you're eating these soft, buttery cookies. Each thumbprint is filled with rich, melt-in-your-mouth chocolate.*

**variation**

Roll the balls in granulated sugar before arranging on cookie sheet.

# Chocolate Tom Thumbs

| | | |
|---|---|---|
| All-purpose flour | 1 3/4 cups | 425 mL |
| Butter (or hard margarine), softened | 1 cup | 250 mL |
| Brown sugar, packed | 1/2 cup | 125 mL |
| Cocoa, sifted if lumpy | 1/4 cup | 60 mL |
| Baking powder | 1/2 tsp. | 2 mL |
| Salt | 1/8 tsp. | 0.5 mL |
| **CHOCOLATE FILLING** | | |
| Icing (confectioner's) sugar | 1 1/4 cups | 300 mL |
| Butter (or hard margarine), softened | 1/4 cup | 60 mL |
| Cocoa, sifted if lumpy | 1/4 cup | 60 mL |
| Water | 2 tbsp. | 30 mL |
| Vanilla extract | 1/2 tsp. | 2 mL |

Combine first 6 ingredients in large bowl. Shape into 1 inch (2.5 cm) balls. Arrange, about 1 inch (2.5 cm) apart, on greased cookie sheets. Dent each ball with thumb. Bake in 325°F (160°C) oven for 5 minutes. Press dents again. Bake for about 10 minutes until firm. Let stand on cookie sheets for 5 minutes. Remove cookies from cookie sheets and place on wire racks to cool. Cool cookie sheets between batches.

**Chocolate Filling:** Beat all 5 ingredients in medium bowl until smooth and fluffy. Makes about 1 cup (250 mL) filling. Fill dents in cookies. Makes about 54 cookies.

*1 cookie: 70 Calories; 4.3 g Total Fat (1.1 g Mono, 0.2 g Poly, 2.7 g Sat); 11 mg Cholesterol; 8 g Carbohydrate; trace Fibre; 1 g Protein; 39 mg Sodium*

Pictured at right.

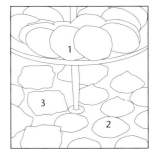

1. Swirling Dervish Cookies, page 40
2. Chocolate Tom Thumbs, above
3. Chocolate Sandwiches, page 41

*These spicy German Christmas cookies (pronounced LAYB-koo-khun) are delicious whether you serve them glazed, decorated or as-is.*

## about lebkuchen

This cake-like cookie is a specialty of Nuremberg, Germany. Lebkuchen are sweetened with honey and generally include spices, citron and almonds, all topped with a sweet glaze. Among the most popular German cookies, lebkuchen have been around for centuries and are often formed into intricate designs and decorative shapes by baking the cookies in special molds. In Germany, you may even see lebkuchen cut into festive shapes and used as Christmas tree ornaments.

# Lebkuchen

| | | |
|---|---|---|
| Liquid honey | 2/3 cup | 150 mL |
| Fancy (mild) molasses | 1/3 cup | 75 mL |
| Large egg | 1 | 1 |
| Brown sugar, packed | 3/4 cup | 175 mL |
| Chopped citron peel | 1/2 cup | 125 mL |
| Finely chopped almonds | 1/3 cup | 75 mL |
| Lemon juice | 2 tbsp. | 30 mL |
| All-purpose flour | 3 1/2 cups | 875 mL |
| Ground cinnamon | 1 tsp. | 5 mL |
| Baking soda | 1/2 tsp. | 2 mL |
| Ground cloves | 1/2 tsp. | 2 mL |
| Ground nutmeg | 1/2 tsp. | 2 mL |
| Salt | 1/2 tsp. | 2 mL |
| Glazed cherries, halved | 21 | 21 |
| Sliced almonds, approximately | 1/3 cup | 75 mL |
| Corn syrup, warmed | 1/4 cup | 60 mL |

Combine honey and molasses in small saucepan. Bring to a boil. Remove from heat.

Beat egg in large bowl until frothy. Beat in brown sugar. Add next 3 ingredients and honey mixture. Stir.

Combine remaining 6 ingredients in small bowl. Add to egg mixture. Mix well. Roll out on lightly floured surface to 1/4 inch (6 mm) thickness. Cut into 2 1/2 inch (6 cm) circles with lightly floured cookie cutter. Arrange on greased cookie sheets.

Put 1 cherry half in centre of each cookie. Arrange almond slices around cherries. Bake in 375°F (190°C) oven for about 8 minutes until firm. Let stand on cookie sheets for 5 minutes.

Brush with corn syrup to glaze. Remove cookies from cookie sheets and place on wire racks to cool. Cool cookie sheets between batches. Makes about 42 cookies.

*1 cookie: 105 Calories; 1.1 g Total Fat (0.7 g Mono, 0.3 g Poly, 0.1 g Sat); 4 mg Cholesterol; 23 g Carbohydrate; 1 g Fibre; 2 g Protein; 54 mg Sodium*

Pictured at right.

# Santa's Whiskers

| | | |
|---|---|---|
| All-purpose flour | 2 1/2 cups | 625 mL |
| Butter (or hard margarine), softened | 1 cup | 250 mL |
| Granulated sugar | 1 cup | 250 mL |
| Finely chopped red and green glazed cherries | 3/4 cup | 175 mL |
| Chopped pecans | 1/2 cup | 125 mL |
| Milk | 2 tbsp. | 30 mL |
| Vanilla extract | 1 tsp. | 5 mL |
| Flaked coconut | 1 cup | 250 mL |

Combine first 7 ingredients in medium bowl. Roll into two 2 inch (5 cm) diameter logs.

Roll in coconut. Wrap in plastic wrap. Chill for several hours or overnight. Discard plastic wrap. Cut into 1/4 inch (6 mm) slices. Arrange on ungreased cookie sheets. Bake in 375°F (190°C) oven for 10 to 12 minutes until edges start to brown. Let stand on cookie sheets for 10 minutes. Remove cookies from cookie sheets and place on wire racks to cool. Cool cookie sheets between batches. Makes about 60 cookies.

*1 cookie: 75 Calories; 4.1 g Total Fat (1.2 g Mono, 0.3 g Poly, 2.3 g Sat); 8 mg Cholesterol; 9 g Carbohydrate; trace Fibre; 1 g Protein; 26 mg Sodium*

Pictured on front cover and below.

*These colourful fruit and nut-filled cookies are edged in shreds of white coconut that look just like Santa's beard. Make these one day and bake them the next.*

Top: Santa's Whiskers, above
Bottom: Lebkuchen, page 44

*Two different-sized cookie cutters are needed to make these cookie cut-outs filled with melted candy. A pretty stained-glass effect is the result. Mix and match the outer and inner cookie cutters for your own unique shapes.*

## tip

To crush hard candies, place in a large resealable freezer bag. Seal the bag and gently hit the candies with the flat side of a meat mallet or rolling pin until crushed to the desired fineness.

# Brown Sugar And Spice

| | | |
|---|---|---|
| Butter (or hard margarine), softened | 1/2 cup | 125 mL |
| Brown sugar, packed | 1 cup | 250 mL |
| Large egg | 1 | 1 |
| All-purpose flour | 2 cups | 500 mL |
| Baking powder | 2 tsp. | 10 mL |
| Ground cinnamon | 2 tsp. | 10 mL |
| Ground nutmeg | 1 tsp. | 5 mL |
| Salt | 1/4 tsp. | 1 mL |
| Crushed hard caramel candies or clear hard candies (see Tip) | 1/4 cup | 60 mL |

Cream butter and brown sugar in large bowl. Add egg. Beat well.

Combine next 5 ingredients in medium bowl. Add to butter mixture in 2 additions, mixing well after each addition, until no dry flour remains. Divide dough in half. Shape each half into slightly flattened disc. Wrap with plastic wrap. Let stand for 30 minutes. Discard plastic wrap from 1 disc. Roll out dough on lightly floured surface to about 1/8 inch (3 mm) thickness. Cut out shapes with lightly floured cookie cutter. Roll out scraps to cut more shapes. Arrange about 2 inches (5 cm) apart on parchment paper-lined cookie sheets. Cut out centre of each cookie with smaller, lightly floured cookie cutter.

Spoon 1/2 tsp. (2 mL) candy into cut-out centre of each cookie (see Note). Bake in 350°F (175°C) oven for 8 to 10 minutes until golden and candy is melted. Let stand on cookie sheets for 10 minutes. Remove cookies from cookie sheets and place on wire racks to cool. Cool cookie sheets between batches. Repeat with remaining disc and candy. Makes about 30 cookies.

*1 cookie: 92 Calories; 3.4 g Total Fat (0.9 g Mono, 0.1 g Poly, 2.1 g Sat); 14 mg Cholesterol; 15 g Carbohydrate; trace Fibre; 1 g Protein; 68 mg Sodium*

**Note:** To save time on cleanup, use a pastry brush to sweep any candy crumbs from the cookie sheet before baking.

Pictured on front cover and at right.

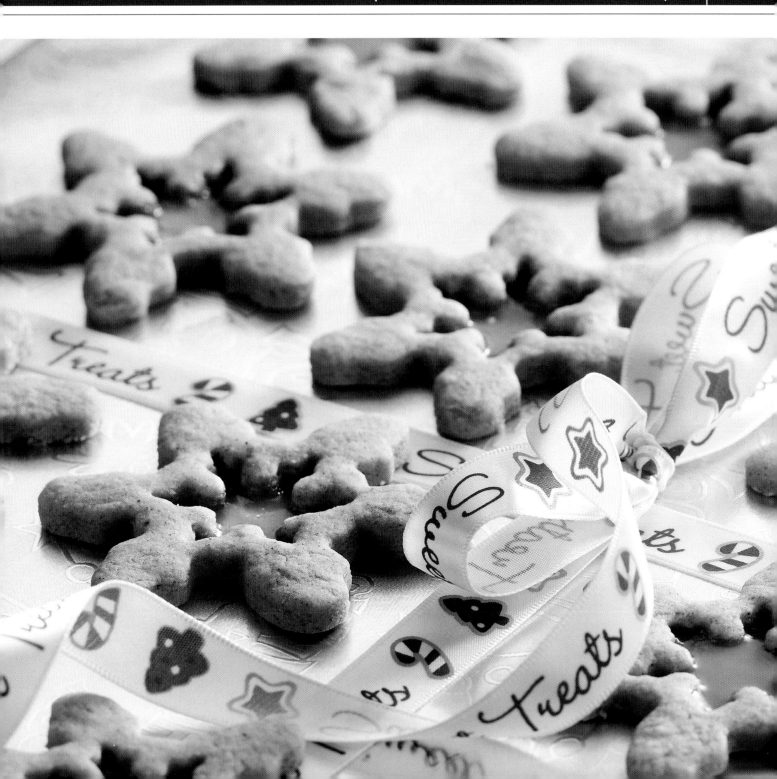

*Two classic Christmas flavours, mandarin orange and chocolate, combine for a deliciously crisp dunking cookie. Serve with coffee or hot chocolate.*

## about biscotti

This favourite Italian cookie's uniquely hard and crunchy texture is perfect for soaking up coffee, cocoa or your favourite hot beverage. Biscotti get their shape from being baked twice—once as bread-like loaves, then again after the loaves are sliced. The second baking toasts the slices, giving them their distinctive crunch. Sometimes biscotti are "dressed to impress" with dips or drizzles of chocolate after this second baking. And the flavour combinations of biscotti are limitless. You're bound to find a variety that perfectly complements your favourite hot drink.

# Mandarin Chocolate Biscotti

| | | |
|---|---|---|
| Butter (or hard margarine), softened | 1/2 cup | 125 mL |
| Granulated sugar | 1 cup | 250 mL |
| Large eggs | 3 | 3 |
| Egg yolk (large) | 1 | 1 |
| Vanilla extract | 1 tsp. | 5 mL |
| All-purpose flour | 4 cups | 1 L |
| Baking powder | 2 1/2 tsp. | 12 mL |
| Salt | 1/4 tsp. | 1 mL |
| Large seedless mandarin oranges, peel reserved | 2 | 2 |
| Coarsely chopped milk chocolate bar | 2/3 cup | 150 mL |
| Finely chopped reserved mandarin orange peel, white pith scraped off | 1 1/2 tbsp. | 25 mL |
| Egg white (large) | 1 | 1 |
| Water | 1 tsp. | 5 mL |
| Granulated sugar | 1 tbsp. | 15 mL |

Cream butter and first amount of sugar in large bowl. Beat in next 3 ingredients.

Combine next 3 ingredients in medium bowl. Add to egg mixture. Stir well.

Separate oranges into sections. Cut each section into 3 or 4 pieces, reserving any juice. Add orange pieces and reserved juice to dough. Mix well. Add chocolate and orange peel. Mix well. Turn out dough onto well-floured surface. Divide dough in half. Shape each half into 11 inch (28 cm) long log. Place, 1 1/2 to 2 inches (3.8 to 5 cm) apart, on ungreased large cookie sheet. Flatten each log slightly.

Whisk egg white and water in small bowl until frothy. Brush over logs. Sprinkle second amount of sugar over top. Bake in 375°F (190°C) oven for 30 minutes until lightly browned. Let stand on cookie sheet for 1 hour until cool. Using serrated knife, cut logs diagonally into 1/2 inch (12 mm) slices. Lay slices, cut side down, on same cookie sheet. Bake in 325°F (160°C) oven for 30 to 35 minutes, turning slices over at halftime, until crisp. Remove to wire racks to cool completely. Makes about 32 biscotti.

*1 biscotti: 131 Calories; 4.5 g Total Fat (1.4 g Mono, 0.2 g Poly, 2.6 g Sat); 31 mg Cholesterol; 21 g Carbohydrate; 1 g Fibre; 3 g Protein; 67 mg Sodium*

Pictured on page 51.

# Cranberry Almond Biscotti

| | | |
|---|---|---|
| All-purpose flour | 1 3/4 cups | 425 mL |
| Granulated sugar | 2/3 cup | 150 mL |
| Baking powder | 1/2 tsp. | 2 mL |
| Salt | 1/4 tsp. | 1 mL |
| Butter (or hard margarine), softened | 1/3 cup | 75 mL |
| Large eggs | 2 | 2 |
| Almond extract | 1/2 tsp. | 2 mL |
| Dried cranberries | 2/3 cup | 150 mL |
| Whole natural almonds | 2/3 cup | 150 mL |

*Traditional biscotti flavour, but in a cute and convenient miniature size! Makes a great gift for coffee lovers—just place in a clear jar and decorate with a festive ribbon.*

Combine first 4 ingredients in large bowl. Cut in butter until mixture resembles coarse crumbs. Make a well in centre.

Beat eggs and extract with fork in small bowl. Add to well. Mix until stiff dough forms. Turn out onto lightly floured surface. Shape dough into ball. Flatten slightly.

Sprinkle cranberries and almonds over top. Press down lightly. Fold dough in half to enclose cranberries and almonds. Knead for 1 to 2 minutes until evenly distributed. Divide dough into 4 equal portions. Roll each portion into 6 inch (15 cm) long log. Place about 2 inches (5 cm) apart on greased cookie sheet. Flatten each log slightly. Bake in 350°F (175°C) oven for about 20 minutes until golden. Let stand on cookie sheet for about 20 minutes until cool enough to handle. Using serrated knife, cut logs diagonally into 1/2 inch (12 mm) slices. Arrange, evenly spaced apart, on greased cookie sheets. Bake in 300°F (150°C) oven for about 20 minutes, turning once at halftime, until dry and crisp. Let stand on cookie sheets for 5 minutes before removing to wire racks to cool. Makes about 42 biscotti.

*1 biscotti: 64 Calories; 2.8 g Total Fat (1.2 g Mono, 0.4 g Poly, 1.1 g Sat); 13 mg Cholesterol; 9 g Carbohydrate; trace Fibre; 1 g Protein; 30 mg Sodium*

Pictured on page 51.

*Stollen (pronounced SHTOH-luhn) is a traditional German Christmas loaf. Here we've transformed it into biscotti for a totally modern take on this festive favourite.*

**tip**

If you'd rather forgo the spiced rum, use 1/2 tsp. (2 mL) rum extract and add orange juice to make 3 tbsp. (50 mL).

# Stollen Tea Dunkers

| | | |
|---|---|---|
| Chopped mixed glazed fruit | 1 cup | 250 mL |
| Sultana raisins | 1/2 cup | 125 mL |
| Spiced rum (see Tip) | 3 tbsp. | 50 mL |
| All-purpose flour | 2 1/2 cups | 625 mL |
| Granulated sugar | 1 cup | 250 mL |
| Sliced natural almonds, toasted (see Tip, page 96) | 3/4 cup | 175 mL |
| Baking powder | 1 tsp. | 5 mL |
| Salt | 1/8 tsp. | 0.5 mL |
| Large eggs | 2 | 2 |
| Butter (or hard margarine), melted | 1/4 cup | 60 mL |
| Grated lemon zest | 1/2 tsp. | 2 mL |
| Icing (confectioner's) sugar, for dusting | | |

Combine glazed fruit and raisins in medium bowl. Add rum. Stir well. Cover. Let stand at room temperature for at least 6 hours or overnight, stirring occasionally.

Combine next 5 ingredients in large bowl. Make a well in centre.

Beat next 3 ingredients in small bowl. Add to well. Add fruit mixture. Mix until stiff dough forms. Turn out onto lightly floured surface. Knead 6 times. Divide dough in half. Roll each half into 12 inch (30 cm) long log. Place, about 2 inches (5 cm) apart, on greased cookie sheet. Flatten each log slightly. Bake in 350°F (175°C) oven for 25 to 30 minutes until golden. Let stand on cookie sheet for about 20 minutes until cool enough to handle. Using a serrated knife, cut logs diagonally into 3/4 inch (2 cm) slices.

Arrange, evenly spaced apart, on same cookie sheet. Bake in 300°F (150°C) oven for about 30 minutes, turning once at halftime, until dry and crisp. Let stand on cookie sheet for 5 minutes before removing to wire rack to cool. Dust half of each slice, on both sides, with icing sugar. Makes about 25 dunkers.

*1 dunker: 152 Calories; 4.4 g Total Fat (2.0 g Mono, 0.7 g Poly, 1.4 g Sat); 20 mg Cholesterol; 26 g Carbohydrate; 1 g Fibre; 3 g Protein; 50 mg Sodium*

Pictured on page 51.

1. Mandarin Chocolate
   Biscotti, page 48
2. Cranberry Almond
   Biscotti, page 49
3. Stollen Tea Dunkers,
   page 50

These Nanaimo bar-type squares have a festive green layer and great minty-chocolate flavour.

# Hint O' Mint Squares

| | | |
|---|---|---|
| Icing (confectioner's) sugar | 1 cup | 250 mL |
| Butter (or hard margarine), softened | 1/4 cup | 60 mL |
| Peppermint extract | 1/2 tsp. | 2 mL |
| Drops of green food colouring | 2 | 2 |
| Butter (or hard margarine) | 1/2 cup | 125 mL |
| Cocoa, sifted if lumpy | 1/4 cup | 60 mL |
| Granulated sugar | 1/4 cup | 60 mL |
| Large egg, fork-beaten | 1 | 1 |
| Chocolate wafer crumbs | 3/4 cup | 175 mL |
| Flaked coconut | 3/4 cup | 175 mL |
| Graham cracker crumbs | 3/4 cup | 175 mL |
| Semi-sweet chocolate chips | 3/4 cup | 175 mL |
| Butter (or hard margarine), melted | 2 1/2 tbsp. | 37 mL |

Beat first 4 ingredients in small bowl until smooth. Press firmly in waxed paper-lined 9 x 9 inch (22 x 22 cm) pan. Freeze until firm.

Combine next 3 ingredients in large saucepan on medium. Heat and stir until sugar is dissolved. Remove from heat. Quickly whisk in egg until thickened slightly.

Add next 3 ingredients. Stir well. Scatter half of crumb mixture into foil-lined 9 x 9 inch (22 x 22 cm) pan. Remove frozen peppermint layer from pan. Turn upside down over crumb mixture. Peel off waxed paper. Scatter remaining half of crumb mixture over peppermint layer. Pack firmly into pan.

Heat chocolate chips and third amount of butter in small heavy saucepan on lowest heat, stirring often, until chocolate is almost melted. Do not overheat. Stir until smooth. Pour over squares. Spread evenly. Let stand until chocolate is firm. Cuts into 36 squares.

*1 square: 104 Calories; 6.8 g Total Fat (1.8 g Mono, 0.4 g Poly, 4.2 g Sat); 17 mg Cholesterol; 11 g Carbohydrate; 1 g Fibre; 1 g Protein; 63 mg Sodium*

Pictured on page 55.

# Bliss Bars

| | | |
|---|---|---|
| Butter (or hard margarine), softened | 3/4 cup | 175 mL |
| Brown sugar, packed | 3/4 cup | 175 mL |
| Large egg | 1 | 1 |
| Vanilla extract | 1 tsp. | 5 mL |
| All-purpose flour | 1 1/3 cups | 325 mL |
| Baking powder | 1/2 tsp. | 2 mL |
| Salt | 1/4 tsp. | 1 mL |
| Semi-sweet chocolate chips | 1 cup | 250 mL |
| Chocolate wafer crumbs | 1/2 cup | 125 mL |
| Butterscotch chips | 1 cup | 250 mL |
| Flaked coconut | 1 1/4 cups | 300 mL |
| Finely chopped pecans | 1/3 cup | 75 mL |
| Can of sweetened condensed milk | 11 oz. | 300 mL |

*A layer of chocolate chip cookie is topped with coconut, pecans and butterscotch chips. The result? Pure bliss!*

Cream butter and brown sugar in large bowl. Add egg. Beat well. Add vanilla. Beat until smooth.

Combine next 3 ingredients in small bowl. Add to butter mixture. Mix until no dry flour remains.

Add chocolate chips. Mix well. Spread evenly in greased 9 x 13 inch (22 x 33 cm) pan.

Sprinkle next 4 ingredients, in order given, over chocolate chip mixture.

Drizzle condensed milk over pecans. Bake in 350°F (175°C) oven for about 25 minutes until edges are golden and topping is set. Cool. Cuts into 36 bars.

*1 bar: 170 Calories; 9.3 g Total Fat (2.4 g Mono, 0.6 g Poly, 5.8 g Sat); 18 mg Cholesterol; 21 g Carbohydrate; 1 g Fibre; 2 g Protein; 82 mg Sodium*

Pictured on page 55.

*With its attractive layers of tan, white and pink, this is a pretty addition to your tray of holiday treats. For easier cutting, make two or three days in advance.*

### tip

If you do not have maraschino cherry juice, substitute 3 tbsp. (50 mL) water with 1 drop of red food coloring and 1/4 tsp. (1 mL) of cherry or almond extract.

# Neapolitan Squares

| BOTTOM LAYER | | |
|---|---|---|
| Butter (or hard margarine) | 1/2 cup | 125 mL |
| Graham cracker crumbs | 1 1/4 cups | 300 mL |
| Brown sugar, packed | 1/2 cup | 125 mL |
| All-purpose flour | 1/3 cup | 75 mL |
| SECOND LAYER | | |
| Medium unsweetened coconut | 2 cups | 500 mL |
| Can of sweetened condensed milk | 11 oz. | 300 mL |
| ICING | | |
| Icing (confectioner's) sugar | 2 cups | 500 mL |
| Butter (or hard margarine), softened | 1/4 cup | 60 mL |
| Maraschino cherry juice (see Tip) | 3 tbsp. | 50 mL |

**Bottom Layer:** Melt butter in medium saucepan. Remove from heat. Add next 3 ingredients. Stir. Press firmly in ungreased 9 x 9 inch (22 x 22 cm) pan. Bake in 350°F (175°C) oven for 10 minutes.

**Second Layer:** Combine coconut and condensed milk in small bowl. Immediately spread over bottom layer. Bake in 350°F (175°C) oven for about 20 minutes until starting to turn golden. Cool.

**Icing:** Beat all 3 ingredients in small bowl, adding more juice if necessary, until spreading consistency. Spread over cooled bars. Let stand, tightly covered, overnight to soften. Cuts into 36 squares.

*1 square: 142 Calories; 7.5 g Total Fat (1.4 g Mono, 0.3 g Poly, 5.3 g Sat); 13 mg Cholesterol; 18 g Carbohydrate; 1 g Fibre; 1 g Protein; 58 mg Sodium*

Pictured at right.

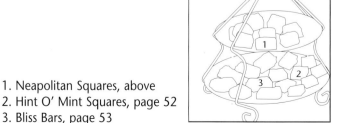

1. Neapolitan Squares, above
2. Hint O' Mint Squares, page 52
3. Bliss Bars, page 53

*This festive treat is filled with the natural sweetness of fruit and honey. Easy to make, and great for holiday gift-giving.*

### about honey

Ancient Egyptians used honey as a form of payment, and the Ancient Greeks used it to make mead—the nectar of the gods. Today, there are over 300 varieties of honey in North America alone. Honey comes in many different colours and flavours, each one based on the type of flower the honeybee colony gets its nectar from. So, if you're a honey lover, step outside the basic supermarket varieties and opt for some blueberry, sourwood or eucalyptus honey. There are enough varieties out there to keep you in honey heaven for a very long time.

*If you're looking for the festive flavour of mincemeat without the fuss of making a pie, try these moist, spicy bars. They're especially good with homemade mincemeat.*

# Fruit And Honey Bars

| | | |
|---|---|---|
| Chopped dried figs | 1 cup | 250 mL |
| Chopped glazed pineapple | 1 cup | 250 mL |
| Coarsely chopped pitted dates | 1 cup | 250 mL |
| Coarsely chopped walnuts | 1 cup | 250 mL |
| Golden raisins | 1 cup | 250 mL |
| Halved red glazed cherries | 1 cup | 250 mL |
| Large eggs | 3 | 3 |
| Liquid honey | 1/2 cup | 125 mL |
| All-purpose flour | 1 1/2 cups | 375 mL |

Combine first 6 ingredients in large bowl.

Beat eggs and honey in small bowl until smooth. Add to fruit mixture. Stir well.

Add flour. Mix well. Spray 9 x 13 inch (22 x 33 cm) pan with cooking spray. Line pan with parchment (not waxed) paper, leaving 1 inch (2.5 cm) overhang on both long sides. Spread fruit mixture evenly in pan. Bake in 325°F (160°C) oven for about 45 minutes until wooden pick inserted in centre comes out clean. Cool. Using parchment paper, remove fruit mixture from pan. Discard parchment paper. Cuts into 64 bars.

*1 bar: 73 Calories; 1.5 g Total Fat (0.3 g Mono, 0.9 g Poly, 0.2 g Sat); 9 mg Cholesterol; 15 g Carbohydrate; 1 g Fibre; 1 g Protein; 8 mg Sodium*

Pictured on front cover and at right.

# Mincemeat Squares

| | | |
|---|---|---|
| All-purpose flour | 1 1/2 cups | 375 mL |
| Butter (or hard margarine), softened | 3/4 cup | 175 mL |
| Brown sugar, packed | 1/2 cup | 125 mL |
| Quick-cooking rolled oats | 1/2 cup | 125 mL |
| Mincemeat | 1 cup | 250 mL |
| Icing (confectioner's) sugar, optional | | |

Stir first 4 ingredients in medium bowl until mixture resembles coarse crumbs. Press 2/3 of mixture in ungreased 9 x 9 inch (22 x 22 cm) pan.

*(continued on next page)*

Process mincemeat in blender until smooth. Spread over oat mixture. Sprinkle remaining oat mixture over mincemeat. Press down lightly, using back of spoon. Bake in 350°F (175°C) oven for 25 to 30 minutes until set and golden. Cool.

Dust with icing sugar. Cuts into 36 squares.

*1 square:* 81 Calories; 4.3 g Total Fat (1.1 g Mono, 0.2 g Poly, 2.6 g Sat); 10 mg Cholesterol; 10 g Carbohydrate; trace Fibre; 1 g Protein; 29 mg Sodium

Pictured below.

Left: Mincemeat Squares, page 56
Right: Fruit And Honey Bars, page 56

*Fancy and festive, the layer of raspberry jam adds some nice colour to these attractive squares.*

# Raspberry Bars

### SHORTBREAD CRUST

| | | |
|---|---|---|
| All-purpose flour | 1 1/4 cups | 300 mL |
| Granulated sugar | 1/4 cup | 60 mL |
| Butter (or hard margarine), softened | 1/2 cup | 125 mL |
| Raspberry jam | 1 cup | 250 mL |

### COCONUT TOPPING

| | | |
|---|---|---|
| Large eggs | 2 | 2 |
| Shredded coconut | 2 cups | 500 mL |
| Granulated sugar | 1 cup | 250 mL |
| All-purpose flour | 1 tbsp. | 15 mL |
| Vanilla extract | 1 tsp. | 5 mL |
| Baking powder | 1/2 tsp. | 2 mL |

**Shortbread Crust:** Combine flour and sugar in medium bowl. Cut in butter until mixture resembles fine crumbs. Press firmly in ungreased 9 x 9 inch (22 x 22 cm) pan. Bake in 350°F (175°C) oven for about 15 minutes until golden.

Spoon jam over crust. Spread carefully.

**Coconut Topping:** Beat eggs in large bowl until frothy. Add remaining 5 ingredients. Stir well. Spread over jam layer. Bake in 350°F (175°C) oven for about 30 minutes until golden. Cool. Cuts into 36 bars.

*1 bar: 115 Calories; 4.6 g Total Fat (0.9 g Mono, 0.2 g Poly, 3.3 g Sat); 17 mg Cholesterol; 18 g Carbohydrate; trace Fibre; 1 g Protein; 39 mg Sodium*

Pictured below.

# Chinese Chews

| | | |
|---|---|---|
| Chopped pitted dates | 1 cup | 250 mL |
| Granulated sugar | 1 cup | 250 mL |
| All-purpose flour | 3/4 cup | 175 mL |
| Chopped walnuts | 1/2 cup | 125 mL |
| Baking powder | 1 tsp. | 5 mL |
| Salt | 1/4 tsp. | 1 mL |
| Large eggs | 2 | 2 |
| Icing (confectioner's) sugar | 2 tbsp. | 30 mL |

*Although no one is quite sure where the name for these squares came from, one thing is certain: they're moist, chewy and always a favourite. They have a rich sweetness from the dates and lots of crunch from the walnuts.*

Combine first 6 ingredients in medium bowl.

Beat eggs in small bowl until thick and pale. Pour over flour mixture. Stir well. Transfer to greased 9 x 9 inch (22 x 22 cm) pan. Bake in 350°F (175°C) oven for about 25 minutes until wooden pick inserted in centre comes out clean. Let stand on wire rack for 10 minutes. Cut into squares while still warm. Let stand in pan until cool.

Dust with icing sugar. Cuts into 36 squares.

*1 square: 58 Calories; 1.4 g Total Fat (0.3 g Mono, 0.8 g Poly, 0.2 g Sat); 10 mg Cholesterol; 11 g Carbohydrate; trace Fibre; 1 g Protein; 27 mg Sodium*

Pictured on page 3 and below.

*With crunchy nuts and a delicious caramel flavour, this not-too-sweet treat is made effortlessly with the use of biscuit mix! Serve alongside traditional chocolate brownies for great flavour and colour contrast.*

# Blondie Brownies

| | | |
|---|---|---|
| Biscuit mix | 2 cups | 500 mL |
| Brown sugar, packed | 1 1/2 cups | 375 mL |
| Large eggs | 3 | 3 |
| Chopped pecans | 1 cup | 250 mL |

Beat first 3 ingredients in large bowl for about 3 minutes until smooth.

Add pecans. Stir. Spread in greased 9 x 9 inch (22 x 22 cm) pan. Bake in 350°F (175°C) oven for about 30 minutes until wooden pick inserted in centre comes out clean. Let stand on wire rack for 10 minutes. Cuts into 36 squares.

*1 square: 117 Calories; 5.0 g Total Fat (2.5 g Mono, 1.0 g Poly, 1.0 g Sat); 16 mg Cholesterol; 17 g Carbohydrate; 1 g Fibre; 2 g Protein; 148 mg Sodium*

Pictured at right.

*These miniature brownies pack a double-dose of chocolate flavour. A moist brownie base is loaded with chocolate chips for a treat that chocolate lovers will go mad for!*

# Double-Chocolate Minis

| | | |
|---|---|---|
| All-purpose flour | 3/4 cup | 175 mL |
| Cocoa, sifted if lumpy | 1/2 cup | 125 mL |
| Salt | 1/4 tsp. | 1 mL |
| Granulated sugar | 1 cup | 250 mL |
| Butter (or hard margarine), melted | 1/3 cup | 75 mL |
| Large eggs | 2 | 2 |
| Semi-sweet chocolate chips | 1 cup | 250 mL |

Preheat oven to 350°F (175°C). Combine first 3 ingredients in small bowl.

Whisk next 3 ingredients in medium bowl until combined. Add flour mixture. Stir well.

Add chocolate chips. Stir. Fill 24 greased and floured mini-muffin cups 3/4 full. Bake for about 15 minutes until wooden pick inserted in centre of brownie comes out moist but not wet with batter. Do not overbake. Makes 24 mini-brownies.

*1 mini-brownie: 109 Calories; 5.3 g Total Fat (1.6 g Mono, 0.2 g Poly, 3.1 g Sat); 22 mg Cholesterol; 16 g Carbohydrate; 1 g Fibre; 2 g Protein; 49 mg Sodium*

Pictured at right.

1. Cream Cheese Brownies, page 62
2. Double-Chocolate Minis, page 60
3. Caramel Chocolate Squares, page 63
4. Blondie Brownies, page 60

*The addition of cream cheese makes ordinary brownies extraordinary. Rich flavour and moist texture—absolutely decadent!*

## about cream cheese

This American invention was hugely popularized by one of its primary uses—as an ingredient in cheesecake. Invented in 1872, cream cheese is known for its smooth texture and mildly tangy flavour. Officially, cream cheese is a soft, unripened cheese that must contain at least 33% milk fat and less than 55% moisture. However, there are numerous varieties of cream cheese available today, from whipped, spreadable varieties that are often flavoured, to the lower-fat versions of the traditional cream cheese. The uses for cream cheese have diversified over the years to include savoury versions as a bagel topping, or as an ingredient in all types of recipes, including Cream Cheese Brownies, where it lends an easily recognizeable and entirely decadent flavour.

# Cream Cheese Brownies

| | | |
|---|---|---|
| Semi-sweet chocolate chips | 2/3 cup | 150 mL |
| Large egg | 1 | 1 |
| Spreadable cream cheese | 8 oz. | 250 g |
| Granulated sugar | 1/3 cup | 75 mL |
| All-purpose flour | 2 tbsp. | 30 mL |
| Vanilla extract | 1/2 tsp. | 2 mL |
| Butter (or hard margarine) | 1/2 cup | 125 mL |
| Cocoa, sifted if lumpy | 1/4 cup | 60 mL |
| Large eggs | 2 | 2 |
| Granulated sugar | 3/4 cup | 175 mL |
| All-purpose flour | 3/4 cup | 175 mL |
| Vanilla extract | 1 tsp. | 5 mL |
| Salt | 1/8 tsp. | 0.5 mL |
| Chopped walnuts | 1/2 cup | 125 mL |
| **CHOCO CREAM CHEESE ICING** | | |
| Semi-sweet chocolate chips | 1/4 cup | 60 mL |
| Block of cream cheese, softened | 4 oz. | 125 g |
| Milk | 1 tbsp. | 15 mL |
| Vanilla extract | 1/2 tsp. | 2 mL |
| Icing (confectioner's) sugar | 2 cups | 500 mL |

Heat chocolate in small heavy saucepan on lowest heat, stirring often, until almost melted. Remove from heat. Stir until smooth.

Beat next 5 ingredients in small bowl until smooth. Fold in melted chocolate.

Combine butter and cocoa in small saucepan. Heat and stir on low until smooth. Cool.

Beat second amount of eggs in medium bowl until frothy. Beat in next 4 ingredients. Add walnuts and cocoa mixture. Stir. Spread about 2/3 cocoa mixture in greased 9 x 9 inch (22 x 22 cm) pan. Spoon dabs of cream cheese mixture over cocoa mixture. Carefully spread in even layer. Drop dabs of remaining cocoa mixture, using about 1/2 tsp. (2 mL) for each, in rows over cream cheese mixture. Bake in 350°F (175°C) oven for 30 to 35 minutes until wooden pick inserted in centre comes out moist but clean. Cool.

*(continued on next page)*

**Choco Cream Cheese Icing:** Heat chocolate in small heavy saucepan on lowest heat, stirring often, until almost melted. Remove from heat. Stir until smooth. Beat next 3 ingredients and melted chocolate in medium bowl. Add icing sugar, 1 cup (250 mL) at a time, beating well after each addition, adding more milk or icing sugar as needed until spreading consistency. Makes about 1 1/2 cups (375 mL) icing. Spread over brownies. Cuts into 36 squares.

*1 square: 153 Calories; 8.7 g Total Fat (2.4 g Mono, 1.1 g Poly, 4.7 g Sat); 33 mg Cholesterol; 18 g Carbohydrate; 1 g Fibre; 2 g Protein; 60 mg Sodium*

Pictured on page 61.

# Caramel Chocolate Squares

| | | |
|---|---|---|
| All-purpose flour | 1 1/4 cups | 300 mL |
| Brown sugar, packed | 1/3 cup | 75 mL |
| Butter (or hard margarine), softened | 1/2 cup | 125 mL |
| Large egg | 1 | 1 |
| Block of light cream cheese, softened | 4 oz. | 125 g |
| Caramel ice cream topping | 3/4 cup | 175 mL |
| Vanilla extract | 1 tsp. | 5 mL |
| Chopped walnuts (or pecans) | 1/2 cup | 125 mL |
| Milk chocolate chips | 1 cup | 250 mL |

*Celebrate the holidays in style with this fabulous combination of buttery shortbread and a creamy caramel filling, topped off with walnuts and chocolate.*

Combine flour and brown sugar in medium bowl. Cut in butter until mixture resembles fine crumbs. Transfer 2/3 cup (150 mL) to small bowl. Press remainder firmly in ungreased 9 x 9 inch (22 x 22 cm) pan.

Beat egg and cream cheese in medium bowl. Add caramel topping and vanilla. Beat. Stir in reserved crumb mixture.

Add walnuts. Stir. Spoon over crust. Bake in 375°F (190°C) oven for about 35 minutes until golden.

Sprinkle with chocolate chips. Let stand until melted. Spread. Cool. Cuts into 36 squares.

*1 square: 117 Calories; 6.0 g Total Fat (0.9 g Mono, 0.9 g Poly, 3.2 g Sat); 13 mg Cholesterol; 14 g Carbohydrate; trace Fibre; 2 g Protein; 59 mg Sodium*

Pictured on page 61.

*What better way to ring in the New Year than with a tart cranberry and raisin pie blanketed in whipped cream?*

# Cranberry Pie

| | | |
|---|---|---|
| Fresh (or frozen, thawed) cranberries | 1 1/2 cups | 375 mL |
| Raisins | 1 cup | 250 mL |
| Granulated sugar | 3/4 cup | 175 mL |
| All-purpose flour | 1 1/2 tbsp. | 25 mL |
| Salt | 1/4 tsp. | 1 mL |
| Boiling water | 1/2 cup | 125 mL |
| Unbaked 9 inch (22 cm) pie shell | 1 | 1 |
| Whipping cream | 1 cup | 250 mL |
| Granulated sugar | 2 tsp. | 10 mL |
| Vanilla extract | 1/2 tsp. | 2 mL |

**Fresh cranberries, for garnish**

Process first 5 ingredients in food processor until combined. Add boiling water. Process until almost smooth.

Transfer to pie shell. Bake on bottom rack in 400°F (205°C) oven for about 20 minutes until set. Cool.

Beat next 3 ingredients in small bowl until stiff peaks form. Spoon over pie. Chill.

Garnish with cranberries. Cuts into 8 wedges.

*1 wedge: 311 Calories; 14.5 g Total Fat (3.0 g Mono, 0.4 g Poly, 8.0 g Sat); 41 mg Cholesterol; 49 g Carbohydrate; 2 g Fibre; 2 g Protein; 161 mg Sodium*

Pictured at right.

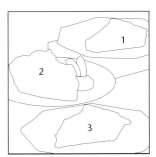

1. Walnut Raisin Tart, page 66
2. Mum's Apple Pie, page 67
3. Cranberry Pie, above

*Definitely not your typical pie. This fancy dessert option has sweet, juicy raisins and tangy sour cream packed into a nut crust. Serve with fresh fruit and whipped cream.*

### tip

Placing the tart pan on a baking sheet provides a safe way to remove the pan from the oven.

### dessert buffet

If you're hosting a larger get-together, you may want to consider a dessert buffet including a number of different sweets, rather than making a large quantity of a single dessert. Just cut each dessert into smaller pieces so that people can sample several sweet treats without overloading on sugar! For example, the Walnut Raisin Tart can be cut into 12 wedges instead of 8.

# Walnut Raisin Tart

## WALNUT CRUST

| | | |
|---|---|---|
| Chopped walnuts | 1 cup | 250 mL |
| All-purpose flour | 3/4 cup | 175 mL |
| Icing (confectioner's) sugar | 1/4 cup | 60 mL |
| Cocoa, sifted if lumpy | 3 tbsp. | 50 mL |
| Cold butter (or hard margarine), cut up | 1/2 cup | 125 mL |

## RAISIN FILLING

| | | |
|---|---|---|
| Sour cream | 1 cup | 250 mL |
| Brown sugar, packed | 1/2 cup | 125 mL |
| Granulated sugar | 1/2 cup | 125 mL |
| Dark raisins | 2/3 cup | 150 mL |
| Chopped walnuts | 1/3 cup | 75 mL |
| Large eggs, fork-beaten | 2 | 2 |
| White vinegar | 1 tbsp. | 15 mL |
| Vanilla extract | 1 tsp. | 5 mL |
| Salt | 1/2 tsp. | 2 mL |
| Ground cinnamon | 1/4 tsp. | 1 mL |
| Ground nutmeg | 1/8 tsp. | 0.5 mL |

**Whipped cream, for garnish**

**Walnut Crust:** Process first 4 ingredients in food processor for 5 seconds. Add butter. Process with on/off motion until mixture resembles fine crumbs. Press in bottom and up side of lightly greased 9 inch (22 cm) tart pan with fluted sides and removable bottom. Place pan on baking sheet (see Tip).

**Raisin Filling:** Combine first 3 ingredients in large bowl. Add next 3 ingredients. Stir.

Add next 5 ingredients. Stir. Spread evenly in pastry shell. Bake on centre rack in 350°F (175°C) oven for about 1 hour until wooden pick inserted in centre comes out clean. Let stand in pan on wire rack until cool. Remove to serving plate.

Garnish with whipped cream. Cuts into 8 wedges.

*1 wedge: 501 Calories; 31.1 g Total Fat (6.9 g Mono, 10.3 g Poly, 12.2 g Sat); 89 mg Cholesterol; 54 g Carbohydrate; 3 g Fibre; 8 g Protein; 264 mg Sodium*

Pictured on page 65.

# Mum's Apple Pie

### SHORTCRUST PASTRY

| | | |
|---|---|---|
| All-purpose flour | 1 3/4 cups | 425 mL |
| Granulated sugar | 1 tbsp. | 15 mL |
| Cold butter (or hard margarine), cut up | 3/4 cup | 175 mL |
| Egg yolk (large), fork-beaten | 1 | 1 |
| Cold water | 2 – 3 tbsp. | 30 – 50 mL |

### FILLING

| | | |
|---|---|---|
| Brown sugar, packed | 1 cup | 250 mL |
| All-purpose flour | 1/2 cup | 125 mL |
| Ground allspice | 1/2 tsp. | 2 mL |
| Ground cinnamon | 1/2 tsp. | 2 mL |
| Ground nutmeg | 1/2 tsp. | 2 mL |
| Ground cloves | 1/4 tsp. | 1 mL |
| Butter (or hard margarine), cut up | 1/2 cup | 125 mL |
| Medium tart cooking apples (such as Granny Smith) | 7 | 7 |

Whipped cream, for garnish
Apple slices, for garnish

*Always a favourite, this apple pie is done the Australian way. Tart, crisp apples with fragrant spices and brown sugar—all nestled in rich, buttery homemade pastry.*

**Shortcrust Pastry:** Combine flour and granulated sugar in large bowl. Cut in butter until smixture resembles coarse crumbs. Add egg yolk. Stir. Add water, 1 tbsp. (15 mL) at a time, stirring after each addition, until soft dough forms. Shape into flattened ball. Wrap with plastic wrap. Chill for 30 minutes. Roll out on lightly floured surface to fit 9 inch (22 cm) deep dish pie plate. Wrap with plastic wrap. Chill for 30 minutes.

**Filling:** Combine first 6 ingredients in large bowl. Cut in butter until mixture resembles coarse crumbs. Sprinkle 1/3 of mixture over pastry.

Peel and core apples. Cut each apple into 8 slices. Arrange over brown sugar layer. Sprinkle remaining brown sugar mixture over apple. Bake on bottom rack in 425°F (220°C) oven for 15 minutes. Reduce heat to 350°F (175°C). Bake for 40 minutes until golden and apples are tender.

Garnish with whipped cream and apple slices. Cuts into 8 wedges.

*1 wedge: 544 Calories; 29.3 g Total Fat (7.7 g Mono, 1.2 g Poly, 18.3 g Sat); 99 mg Cholesterol; 70 g Carbohydrate; 4 g Fibre; 4 g Protein; 215 mg Sodium*

Pictured on page 65.

*Are visions of sugarplums dancing in your head? Moist, dark plums are even more delicious when nestled in a delicate marzipan-like filling.*

# Plum And Almond Tart

### SWEET BUTTER CRUST

| | | |
|---|---|---|
| All-purpose flour | 1 1/2 cups | 375 mL |
| Granulated sugar | 1/4 cup | 60 mL |
| Baking powder | 1/2 tsp. | 2 mL |
| Salt | 1/4 tsp. | 1 mL |
| Cold butter, cut up | 1/2 cup | 125 mL |
| Egg yolks (large) | 2 | 2 |
| Milk | 2 tbsp. | 30 mL |

### ALMOND FILLING

| | | |
|---|---|---|
| Ground almonds | 1 cup | 250 mL |
| Cold butter, cut up | 1/2 cup | 125 mL |
| Granulated sugar | 1/2 cup | 125 mL |
| All-purpose flour | 1/4 cup | 60 mL |
| Egg whites (large) | 2 | 2 |
| Almond extract | 1/2 tsp. | 2 mL |
| Cans of plums in heavy syrup (14 oz., 398 mL, each), drained (or fresh prune plums, enough to cover) | 3 | 3 |
| Sliced almonds, toasted (see Tip, page 96) | 1/3 cup | 75 mL |
| Sanding (decorating) sugar (see Tip, page 84) | 1 tbsp. | 15 mL |

**Sweet Butter Crust:** Process first 4 ingredients in food processor for 5 seconds. Add butter. Process with on/off motion for about 15 seconds until mixture resembles fine crumbs.

*(continued on next page)*

Beat egg yolks and milk with fork in small cup. With food processor motor running, add egg yolk mixture through feed chute until well combined and dough can be formed into ball. Shape dough into slightly flattened disc. Wrap with plastic wrap. Chill for 1 hour. Roll out pastry on lightly floured surface to about 1/8 inch (3 mm) thickness. Press into bottom and up side of lightly greased 10 inch (25 cm) tart pan with fluted side and removable bottom. Trim edge. Chill for 1 hour. Place pan on baking sheet (see Tip, page 66). Cover pastry with parchment paper, bringing paper up over edge. Fill halfway up side with dried beans. Bake on bottom rack in 375°F (190°C) oven for 15 minutes. Carefully remove paper and beans, reserving beans for next time you bake pastry. Let stand on wire rack until cool.

**Almond Filling:** Put first 6 ingredients into same food processor. Process with on/off motion until paste forms. Spoon almond mixture into tart shell. Spread evenly.

Cut plums in half lengthwise and remove pits. Blot dry. Arrange plums, cut-side up and overlapping, in single layer in concentric circles over almond mixture until covered.

Sprinkle with sliced almonds and sanding sugar. Bake on bottom rack in 350°F (175°C) oven for about 45 minutes until crust is golden and filling is evenly raised across top. Filling may still wobble in centre but will set upon cooling. Cuts into 8 wedges.

*1 wedge: 622 Calories; 33.2 g Total Fat (12.3 g Mono, 3.3 g Poly, 15.5 g Sat); 108 mg Cholesterol; 77 g Carbohydrate; 5 g Fibre; 9 g Protein; 298 mg Sodium*

Pictured below.

*Whether your weakness is brownies, caramel or chocolate, you're bound to swoon over this delightful dessert. Add a little whipped cream for a nice finishing touch.*

## presentation idea

Sometimes it's not what you do, but how you do it. Create a fancier presentation by dusting icing sugar in a pattern over the surface of the tart. Cut 12 strips of thick paper, 1/2 inch (12 mm) wide and 10 inches (25 cm) long. Arrange 6 strips, 1 inch (2.5 cm) apart, across the tart in one direction and the remaining 6 strips across the tart in the opposite direction to form diamond shapes. Then dust with icing sugar. Be sure to remove the paper strips carefully in order to keep your pattern intact.

## tip

The caramel is the right consistency when you lift it with a spoon and, as it falls back into the saucepan, it holds a ribbon-like shape on the surface for a few seconds.

# Caramel Brownie Tart

| PROCESSOR PECAN PASTRY | | |
| --- | --- | --- |
| All-purpose flour | 1 cup | 250 mL |
| Cold butter (or hard margarine), cut up | 1/2 cup | 125 mL |
| Icing sugar | 1/4 cup | 60 mL |
| Finely chopped pecans | 1/2 cup | 125 mL |
| Egg yolks (large) | 2 | 2 |
| Cold water | 1 tbsp. | 15 mL |
| CARAMEL FILLING | | |
| Can of sweetened condensed milk | 11 oz. | 300 mL |
| Butter (or hard margarine) | 1/3 cup | 75 mL |
| Whipping cream | 3 tbsp. | 50 mL |
| Brown sugar, packed | 2 tbsp. | 30 mL |
| BROWNIE TOPPING | | |
| Granulated sugar | 1/2 cup | 125 mL |
| Butter (or hard margarine) | 1/3 cup | 75 mL |
| Semi-sweet chocolate baking squares (1 oz., 28 g, each), chopped | 3 | 3 |
| Large egg | 1 | 1 |
| All-purpose flour | 1/3 cup | 75 mL |
| Cocoa, sifted if lumpy | 2 tbsp. | 30 mL |

Icing sugar, for dusting

**Processor Pecan Pastry:** Process first 3 ingredients in food processor until mixture is crumbly.

Add pecans. Process with on/off motion 2 to 3 times until combined. Add egg yolks and cold water. Process until dough forms a ball. Shape into slightly flattened disc. Wrap with plastic wrap. Chill for 30 minutes. Roll out on lightly floured surface to fit 10 inch (25 cm) tart pan with fluted sides and removable bottom. Line tart pan with pastry. Wrap with plastic wrap. Chill for 30 minutes. Place pan on baking sheet (see Tip, page 66). Cover pastry with parchment paper, bringing paper up over edge. Fill halfway up side with dried beans. Bake on bottom rack in 375°F (190°C) oven for 10 minutes. Carefully remove paper and beans, reserving beans for next time you bake pastry. Bake for another 10 minutes until pastry crust is golden around edges. Let stand on wire rack until cool.

*(continued on next page)*

**Caramel Filling:** Combine all 4 ingredients in large saucepan. Heat and stir on medium for about 10 minutes until mixture is pale caramel colour and thick enough to ribbon (see Tip). Cool slightly until thick enough to spread. Spoon into baked pastry crust. Spread evenly. Let stand for about 30 minutes until set.

**Brownie Topping:** Combine granulated sugar and butter in medium saucepan. Heat and stir on medium low until butter is melted and mixture is hot but not boiling. Remove from heat. Add chocolate. Stir until melted.

Add next 3 ingredients. Mix well. Spread over Caramel Filling. Bake in 350°F (175°C) oven for 25 to 30 minutes until just set. Cool in tart pan. Chill, covered, for at least 2 hours or overnight.

Remove from tart pan. Dust with icing sugar. Serve at room temperature. Cuts into 10 wedges.

*1 wedge: 512 Calories; 32.7 g Total Fat (10.2 g Mono, 2.6 g Poly, 17.7 g Sat); 129 mg Cholesterol; 52 g Carbohydrate; 1 g Fibre; 7 g Protein; 201 mg Sodium*

Pictured below.

*Let's not mince words—mincemeat tarts are the tastiest of holiday traditions, especially when served warm with ice cream.*

# Mince Tarts

| | | |
|---|---|---|
| Mincemeat (see Tip) | 2 cups | 500 mL |
| Unsweetened applesauce | 3/4 cup | 175 mL |
| Minute tapioca | 1 1/2 tbsp. | 25 mL |
| Unbaked tart shells | 24 | 24 |
| Frozen mini tart shells, thawed (see Note) | 24 | 24 |
| Large egg, fork-beaten | 1 | 1 |
| Granulated sugar | 1 tsp. | 5 mL |

Combine first 3 ingredients in small bowl.

Fill tart shells with mincemeat mixture about 3/4 full. Dampen edges of pastry with water. Remove mini tart shells from liners. Roll out flat. Set over mincemeat. Press edges to seal.

Brush each with egg. Sprinkle with sugar. Cut small vents in top of each to allow steam to escape. Arrange on ungreased baking sheet. Bake on bottom rack in 400°F (205°C) oven for about 15 minutes until golden. Transfer to wire racks to cool. Makes 24 tarts.

*1 tart: 236 Calories; 13.1 g Total Fat (6.1 g Mono, 1.5 g Poly, 4.5 g Sat); 9 mg Cholesterol; 28 g Carbohydrate; 1 g Fibre; 2 g Protein; 235 mg Sodium*

Pictured at right.

**Note:** Rather than mini tart shells, you can roll out pie pastry and cut circles to fit the tops of your tarts.

*These tiny, tangy tarts have a festive and colourful red filling. Dress them up with a little whipped cream or a dusting of icing sugar.*

# Cranapple Tarts

| | | |
|---|---|---|
| Small peeled cooking apples (such as McIntosh), cut up | 2 | 2 |
| Fresh (or frozen, thawed) cranberries | 2 cups | 500 mL |
| White corn syrup | 1 cup | 250 mL |
| Unbaked tart shells | 24 | 24 |
| Icing (confectioner's) sugar, for garnish whipped cream, for garnish | | |

*(continued on next page)*

Process first 3 ingredients in blender or food processor until cranberries are finely chopped. Transfer to medium bowl.

Arrange tart shells on ungreased baking sheet. Spoon fruit mixture into shells. Bake on bottom rack in 400°F (205°C) oven for about 15 minutes until pastry is golden and filling is bubbling. Transfer to wire racks to cool.

Garnish with icing sugar or whipped cream. Makes 24 tarts.

*1 tart:* 134 Calories; 5.6 g Total Fat (2.4 g Mono, 2.1 g Poly, 0.8 g Sat); 0 mg Cholesterol; 21 g Carbohydrate; 1 g Fibre; 1 g Protein; 122 mg Sodium

Pictured on front cover and below.

1. Cranapple Tarts, page 72
2. Mince Tarts, page 72
3. Jam Tarts, page 74
4. Butter Tarts, page 74

*A Canadian Christmas tradition you'll be pleased to share with any guests visiting from afar.*

# Butter Tarts

| | | |
|---|---|---|
| Brown sugar, packed | 1/2 cup | 125 mL |
| Corn syrup | 1/2 cup | 125 mL |
| Butter (or hard margarine), softened | 3 tbsp. | 50 mL |
| Large egg, fork-beaten | 1 | 1 |
| Raisins (or currants) | 1/2 cup | 125 mL |
| Finely chopped pecans | 2 tbsp. | 30 mL |
| Medium unsweetened coconut | 2 tbsp. | 30 mL |
| White vinegar | 1 1/2 tsp. | 7 mL |
| Salt, just a pinch | | |
| Unbaked tart shells | 12 | 12 |

Combine first 3 ingredients in medium bowl.

Add next 6 ingredients. Mix well.

Arrange tart shells on ungreased baking sheet. Spoon raisin mixture into shells. Bake on bottom rack in 400°F (205°C) oven for about 15 minutes until pastry is golden and filling is bubbling. Transfer to wire racks to cool. Makes 12 tarts.

*1 tart: 225 Calories; 10.2 g Total Fat (3.8 g Mono, 2.5 g Poly, 3.3 g Sat); 23 mg Cholesterol; 34 g Carbohydrate; 1 g Fibre; 2 g Protein; 160 mg Sodium*

Pictured on front cover and page 73.

*With only three ingredients, festive baking couldn't be any easier!*

# Jam Tarts

| | | |
|---|---|---|
| Unbaked tart shells | 12 | 12 |
| Raspberry jam | 3/4 cup | 175 mL |
| Apricot jam | 3/4 cup | 175 mL |

Arrange tart shells on ungreased baking sheet.

Spread raspberry jam evenly in 6 tart shells. Spread apricot jam evenly in remaining tart shells. Bake on bottom rack in 375°F (190°C) oven for about 20 minutes until pastry is golden and filling is bubbling. Transfer to wire racks to cool. Makes 12 tarts.

*1 tart: 185 Calories; 5.6 g Total Fat (2.4 g Mono, 2.1 g Poly, 0.8 g Sat); 0 mg Cholesterol; 34 g Carbohydrate; trace Fibre; 1 g Protein; 117 mg Sodium*

Pictured on page 73.

# Pastry Triangles With Pears

| | | |
|---|---|---|
| Package of puff pastry (14 oz., 397 g), thawed according to package directions | 1/2 | 1/2 |
| Egg yolk (large), fork-beaten | 1 | 1 |
| Sliced almonds | 1/4 cup | 60 mL |
| **CARAMELIZED PEARS** | | |
| Butter (or hard margarine) | 1/3 cup | 75 mL |
| Peeled medium pears, cut into 1/8 inch (3 mm) slices | 4 | 4 |
| Brown sugar, packed | 1/4 cup | 60 mL |
| Dark rum (or 1/2 tsp., 2 mL, rum extract plus water to make) | 2 tbsp. | 30 mL |
| Maple (or maple-flavoured) syrup | 2 tbsp. | 30 mL |
| Ground cinnamon | 3/4 tsp. | 4 mL |

Icing (confectioner's) sugar, for garnish
Whipped cream, for garnish

Roll out pastry on lightly floured surface to 8 x 8 inch (20 x 20 cm) square. Cut into quarters. Cut each quarter into 2 triangles. Arrange about 1/2 inch (12 mm) apart on ungreased baking sheet.

Brush with egg yolk. Sprinkle with almonds. Bake in 400°F (205°C) oven for about 15 minutes until golden. Let stand on baking sheet for 5 minutes before removing to wire rack to cool.

**Caramelized Pears:** Melt butter in large frying pan on medium-low. Add next 5 ingredients. Heat and stir for about 15 minutes until pear is soft and sauce is thickened. Split each triangle in half horizontally into 2 layers. Place bottom half of 1 triangle on individual serving plate. Top with 1/8 of pear mixture. Cover with top half of triangle. Repeat with remaining triangles and pear mixture.

Sprinkle with icing sugar. Serve with whipped cream. Serves 8.

*1 serving: 334 Calories; 20.4 g Total Fat (9.0 g Mono, 2.1 g Poly, 7.6 g Sat); 44 mg Cholesterol; 35 g Carbohydrate; 3 g Fibre; 4 g Protein; 121 mg Sodium*

Pictured on page 77.

*Making a sophisticated dessert is easier than you thought possible! Spiced caramelized pears are served over crisp puff pastry and dusted with icing sugar for a spectacular presentation.*

## christmas fun

You and a friend hold either end of a decorated paper cylinder in your hands and pull—snap! You've just pulled a Christmas cracker, and you're carrying on a tradition that's been around since 1847, when a British confectioner named Tom Smith decided to make paper-wrapped bonbons more exciting by adding a tiny explosive charge! The candy was soon replaced with the now-standard fillings of paper jokes or fortunes, tiny toys and paper hats. Over the years, Christmas crackers have held everything from plastic toys to expensive jewellery, but one thing hasn't changed—that distinctive and startling noise!

*Using crisp phyllo pastry in place of a heavy crust makes for a unique spin on apple pie. Delicious, and with the added bonus of being much lower in fat!*

## about tapioca

If you get a little confused by pie recipes calling for tapioca, you're probably thinking of pearl tapioca—tiny balls of starch from the cassava plant. While pearl tapioca makes for some very tasty pudding, it won't do much for your pie. For pie recipes, you're looking for minute tapioca, also known as quick-cooking or instant tapioca. Minute tapioca is granulated and works much like cornstarch, which is why it is used as a thickener for sauces, glazes and fillings.

# Apples In A Phyllo Crust

| | | |
|---|---|---|
| Peeled cooking apples (such as McIntosh), cored and sliced into thin wedges | 6 | 6 |
| Brown sugar, packed | 1 cup | 250 mL |
| Lemon juice | 2 tbsp. | 30 mL |
| Minute tapioca | 2 tbsp. | 30 mL |
| Ground cinnamon | 1/2 tsp. | 2 mL |
| Phyllo pastry sheets, thawed according to package directions | 3 | 3 |
| Cooking oil | 2 tsp. | 10 mL |
| Graham cracker crumbs | 1/4 cup | 60 mL |
| Cooking oil | 2 tsp. | 10 mL |
| Granulated sugar | 2 tsp. | 10 mL |
| Ground cinnamon | 1/4 tsp. | 1 mL |

Combine first 5 ingredients in large saucepan. Let stand for 10 minutes. Heat and stir on medium until sugar is dissolved and apples are tender-crisp. Cool.

Lightly brush each pastry sheet with cooking oil. Fold in half lengthwise. Sprinkle with graham crumbs.

Centre pastry sheets, crumb-side up, spiral-fashion in ungreased 10 inch (25 cm) glass pie plate, leaving overhang (see diagram 1). Spoon apple filling over pastry sheets (see diagram 2). Fold overhanging pastry sheets over filling (see diagram 3). Brush lightly with second amount of cooking oil.

Combine sugar and second amount of cinnamon in small cup. Sprinkle over pastry. Bake on bottom rack in 350°F (175°C) oven for about 30 minutes until golden. Cool. Cuts into 8 wedges.

*1 wedge: 215 Calories; 2.0 g Total Fat (1.0 g Mono, 0.6 g Poly, 0.3 g Sat); 0 mg Cholesterol; 51 g Carbohydrate; 3 g Fibre; 1 g Protein; 62 mg Sodium*

Pictured at right.

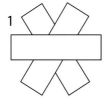
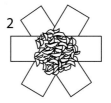

Top: Pastry Triangles With Pears, page 75
Bottom: Apples In A Phyllo Crust, page 76

*Eggnog is undeniably a holiday favourite. Here, we've packed a double-dose of eggnog flavour into a festive steamed pudding. Not only is there eggnog in the pudding, it's also topped with a rich, creamy eggnog sauce.*

# Chocolate Eggnog Pudding

| | | |
|---|---|---|
| Large egg | 1 | 1 |
| Granulated sugar | 1/3 cup | 75 mL |
| Eggnog | 1/2 cup | 125 mL |
| Butter (or hard margarine), melted | 2 tbsp. | 30 mL |
| Brandy (or vanilla) extract | 1/2 tsp. | 2 mL |
| All-purpose flour | 1 cup | 250 mL |
| Cocoa, sifted if lumpy | 2 tbsp. | 30 mL |
| Baking powder | 2 tsp. | 10 mL |
| Ground cinnamon | 1/4 tsp. | 1 mL |
| Ground nutmeg | 1/4 tsp. | 1 mL |
| Salt | 1/4 tsp. | 1 mL |
| **EGGNOG SAUCE** | | |
| Eggnog | 1/2 cup | 125 mL |
| White chocolate baking squares (1 oz., 28 g, each), chopped | 4 | 4 |
| Brandy (or 1/8 tsp., 0.5 mL brandy extract) | 1 tbsp. | 15 mL |

Beat egg and sugar in medium bowl until thick and pale. Set aside.

Combine next 3 ingredients in small bowl. Set aside.

Combine next 6 ingredients in separate medium bowl. Add to egg mixture in 3 additions, alternating with eggnog mixture in 2 additions, until no dry flour remains. Transfer to well-greased 4 cup (1 L) pudding container or heatproof bowl. Bowl should be about 2/3 full. Cover with greased foil. Place on wire rack set in small roasting pan. Pour boiling water into roasting pan until halfway up side of container. Bake in 350°F (175°C) oven for about 50 minutes until wooden pick inserted in centre comes out clean. Carefully remove container from water. Let stand in container for 5 minutes. Invert pudding onto wire rack to cool. Cuts into 8 wedges.

**Eggnog Sauce:** Heat eggnog and white chocolate in small heavy saucepan on lowest heat, stirring often, until chocolate is almost melted. Remove from heat. Stir until smooth. Add brandy. Stir well. Makes about 3/4 cup (175 mL) sauce. Serve with pudding. Serves 8.

*1 serving: 228 Calories; 8.2 g Total Fat (2.5 g Mono, 0.5 g Poly, 4.7 g Sat); 49 mg Cholesterol; 35 g Carbohydrate; 1 g Fibre; 4 g Protein; 184 mg Sodium*

Pictured on page 79.

*Based on the ever-popular English sticky toffee pudding, this cake-like pudding is drizzled with a deliciously buttery caramel sauce. Best served warm.*

### about christmas puddings

The traditional Christmas pudding served by the English is a plum pudding. This is generally a round, solid cake that is boiled. Traditionally, it was served in flaming brandy and garnished with a sprig of holly. The origins of plum pudding date back to medieval times, where it was a porridge made from meat and fruit. Plums were so frequently used that all fruits used in puddings eventually became known as plums. Over time, thickeners were added and the solid plum pudding of today became the standard.

# Sticky Date Pudding

| | | |
|---|---|---|
| Water | 1 1/3 cups | 325 mL |
| Chopped pitted dates | 1 1/3 cups | 325 mL |
| Baking soda | 1 tsp. | 5 mL |
| Large eggs | 2 | 2 |
| All-purpose flour | 1 cup | 250 mL |
| Brown sugar, packed | 3/4 cup | 175 mL |
| Butter (or hard margarine), softened | 1/3 cup | 75 mL |
| Baking powder | 2 tsp. | 10 mL |
| Ground cinnamon | 1 tsp. | 5 mL |
| **WARM CARAMEL SAUCE** | | |
| Brown sugar, packed | 1/2 cup | 125 mL |
| Butter (or hard margarine) | 1/2 cup | 125 mL |
| Whipping cream | 1/2 cup | 125 mL |

Bring water to a boil in medium saucepan. Add dates. Stir. Remove from heat. Add baking soda. Stir. Let stand for 10 minutes. Stir. Pour into large bowl.

Add next 6 ingredients. Beat until well combined. Pour into greased and parchment paper-lined 8 inch (20 cm) springform pan. Bake in 350°F (175°C) oven for about 50 minutes until wooden pick inserted in centre comes out clean. Let stand in pan for 10 minutes. Remove pudding from pan and place on wire rack to cool. Cuts into 8 wedges.

**Warm Caramel Sauce:** Combine all 3 ingredients in large saucepan. Heat and stir on medium for 3 to 5 minutes until butter is melted. Bring to a boil. Boil for about 5 minutes, without stirring, until slightly thickened. Makes about 1 cup (250 mL) sauce. Serve with pudding. Serves 8.

*1 serving: 495 Calories; 25.4 g Total Fat (7.0 g Mono, 1.1 g Poly, 15.6 g Sat); 116 mg Cholesterol; 67 g Carbohydrate; 2 g Fibre; 4 g Protein; 391 mg Sodium*

Pictured at right.

1. Caramel Nut Pudding, page 82
2. Apple Croissant Pudding, page 83
3. Bread Pudding, page 82
4. Sticky Date Pudding, above

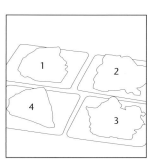

*Transform stale bread into a deliciously rich pudding! This old-time favourite is best served with a scoop of ice cream.*

## queen of puddings

For a truly decadent pudding, use 3 egg yolks in place of whole eggs. Bake as directed. After baking, increase heat to 400°F (200°C). Beat 3 egg whites with 1/4 tsp. (1 mL) cream of tartar until soft peaks form. Add 3 tbsp. (50 mL) granulated sugar, beating constantly, until stiff peaks form. Spread over pudding and bake for another 5 minutes until browned.

*Comfort food is at its best with sweet caramel and crunchy nuts. Use dark brown sugar to ensure a rich, golden caramel in this warming winter treat.*

# Bread Pudding

| | | |
|---|---|---|
| Milk | 2 cups | 500 mL |
| Stale bread cubes | 2 cups | 500 mL |
| Butter (or hard margarine) | 1/4 cup | 60 mL |
| Large eggs, fork-beaten | 2 | 2 |
| Raisins (or currants) | 1 cup | 250 mL |
| Granulated sugar | 1/3 cup | 75 mL |
| Vanilla extract | 1 tsp. | 5 mL |
| Ground cinnamon (or nutmeg) | 1/2 tsp. | 2 mL |
| Salt | 1/2 tsp. | 2 mL |

Heat milk in heavy saucepan on medium for about 5 minutes until very hot and bubbles form around edge of saucepan. Add bread cubes and butter. Stir. Remove from heat.

Add remaining 6 ingredients. Stir. Transfer to 8 inch (20 cm) casserole. Bake, uncovered, in 350°F (175°C) oven for about 45 minutes until set. Serves 6.

*1 serving: 286 Calories; 10.6 g Total Fat (3.1 g Mono, 0.7 g Poly, 5.9 g Sat); 87 mg Cholesterol; 43 g Carbohydrate; 2 g Fibre; 7 g Protein; 395 mg Sodium*

Pictured on page 81.

# Caramel Nut Pudding

| | | |
|---|---|---|
| All-purpose flour | 3/4 cup | 175 mL |
| Chopped pecans, toasted (see Tip, page 96) | 1/3 cup | 75 mL |
| Chopped slivered almonds, toasted (see Tip, page 96) | 1/3 cup | 75 mL |
| Baking powder | 1 1/2 tsp. | 7 mL |
| Salt | 1/4 tsp. | 1 mL |
| Can of sweetened condensed milk | 11 oz. | 300 mL |
| Milk | 2/3 cup | 150 mL |
| Butter (or hard margarine) | 2 tbsp. | 30 mL |
| Vanilla extract | 1 tsp. | 5 mL |
| Dark brown sugar, packed | 1 1/4 cups | 300 mL |
| Boiling water | 2 cups | 500 mL |

Combine first 5 ingredients in large bowl. Make a well in centre.

*(continued on next page)*

Combine next 4 ingredients in medium saucepan. Heat and stir on medium for about 5 minutes until butter is melted. Add to well. Stir until just moistened. Spread evenly in greased 2 quart (2 L) casserole.

Sprinkle with brown sugar. Carefully pour boiling water over pudding. Bake, uncovered, in 350°F (175°C) oven for 25 to 30 minutes until just firm. Let stand for 10 minutes. Serves 6.

*1 serving: 529 Calories; 17.3 g Total Fat (7.6 g Mono, 2.7 g Poly, 6.1 g Sat); 29 mg Cholesterol; 88 g Carbohydrate; 2 g Fibre; 9 g Protein; 290 mg Sodium*

Pictured on page 81.

# Apple Croissant Pudding

| | | |
|---|---|---|
| Chopped dried apple | 2/3 cup | 150 mL |
| Medium croissants, day-old | 4 | 4 |
| Apple jelly | 1/3 cup | 75 mL |
| Large eggs | 4 | 4 |
| Milk | 2 cups | 500 mL |
| Whipping cream | 2 cups | 500 mL |
| Granulated sugar | 2/3 cup | 150 mL |
| Brandy (or 2 tsp., 10 mL, brandy extract) | 3 tbsp. | 30 mL |
| Ground cinnamon, sprinkle | | |
| Icing (confectioner's) sugar, optional | | |

*Bread pudding fans, take note—we've replaced bread with day-old croissants for a crisp, buttery and flaky update on this hearty dessert. The tangy flavour of apple is the perfect match.*

Scatter apple in greased 2 quart (2 L) shallow baking dish.

Cut croissants in half horizontally. Spread jelly on cut sides. Leave as is or cut each half into 3 equal pieces. Arrange, jelly-side up and slightly overlapping, over apple.

Whisk next 5 ingredients in large bowl or 8 cup (2 L) liquid measure. Carefully pour half of cream mixture over croissant pieces. Let stand for 10 minutes.

Stir remaining cream mixture. Carefully pour over croissant pieces. Sprinkle with cinnamon. Set dish in larger baking pan. Slowly pour boiling water into pan until halfway up side of dish. Bake, uncovered, in 325°F (160°C) oven for 1 1/2 to 1 3/4 hours until set and knife inserted in centre comes out clean. Remove dish from pan. Let stand for 20 minutes before serving.

Dust individual servings with icing sugar. Serves 8.

*1 serving: 519 Calories; 29.9 g Total Fat (8.9 g Mono, 1.4 g Poly, 17.4 g Sat); 192 mg Cholesterol; 52 g Carbohydrate; 2 g Fibre; 9 g Protein; 386 mg Sodium*

Pictured on page 81.

Use coloured sanding sugar to make these muffins an even more colourful holiday treat. Tart cranberries are a wonderful contrast to the sweetness. These are great for a Christmas brunch.

### tip

Sanding sugar is a coarse decorating sugar that comes in white and various colours and is available at specialty kitchen stores.

# Cranberry Sparkle Muffins

| Ingredient | Imperial | Metric |
|---|---|---|
| All-purpose flour | 2 cups | 500 mL |
| Baking powder | 1 tbsp. | 15 mL |
| Salt | 1/2 tsp. | 2 mL |
| Butter (or hard margarine), softened | 1/4 cup | 60 mL |
| Granulated sugar | 1/2 cup | 125 mL |
| Large eggs | 2 | 2 |
| Vanilla (or plain) yogurt | 1 cup | 250 mL |
| Chopped fresh (or frozen) cranberries | 1 cup | 250 mL |
| Sanding (decorating) sugar (see Tip) | 2 tbsp. | 30 mL |

Measure first 3 ingredients into large bowl. Stir. Make a well in centre.

Cream butter and granulated sugar in medium bowl. Add eggs, 1 at a time, beating well after each addition. Add yogurt. Stir. Add to well.

Add cranberries. Stir until just moistened. Fill 12 greased muffin cups 3/4 full.

Combine sanding sugar and cinnamon in small cup. Sprinkle on batter. Bake in 375°F (190°C) oven for 18 to 20 minutes until wooden pick inserted in centre of muffin comes out clean. Let stand in pan for 5 minutes before removing to wire rack to cool. Makes 12 muffins.

*1 muffin: 170 Calories; 4.9 g Total Fat (1.3 g Mono, 0.3 g Poly, 2.8 g Sat); 42 mg Cholesterol; 28 g Carbohydrate; 1 g Fibre; 4 g Protein; 213 mg Sodium*

Pictured at right.

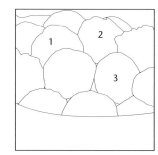

1. Cranberry Sparkle Muffins, above
2. Mocha Hazelnut Muffins, page 86
3. Rummy Eggnog Muffins, page 87

*The perfect blend of flavours—chocolate, hazelnut and coffee go so well together! A hint of allspice rounds out the flavours.*

# Mocha Hazelnut Muffins

| | | |
|---|---|---|
| All-purpose flour | 2 cups | 500 mL |
| Brown sugar, packed | 1 cup | 250 mL |
| Cocoa, sifted if lumpy | 1 tbsp. | 15 mL |
| Instant coffee granules, crushed to fine powder | 1 tbsp. | 15 mL |
| Baking powder | 2 tsp. | 10 mL |
| Baking soda | 1/2 tsp. | 2 mL |
| Ground allspice | 1/2 tsp. | 2 mL |
| Salt | 1/2 tsp. | 2 mL |
| Chocolate milk | 1 cup | 250 mL |
| Butter (or hard margarine), melted | 1/4 cup | 60 mL |
| Large eggs | 2 | 2 |
| Flaked hazelnuts (filberts) | 1/2 cup | 125 mL |
| Flaked hazelnuts (filberts) | 2 tbsp. | 30 mL |

Measure first 8 ingredients into large bowl. Stir. Make a well in centre.

Combine next 3 ingredients in medium bowl. Add to well.

Add first amount of hazelnuts. Stir until just moistened. Fill 12 greased muffin cups 3/4 full.

Sprinkle with second amount of hazelnuts. Bake in 375°F (190°C) oven for 18 to 20 minutes until wooden pick inserted in centre of muffin comes out clean. Let stand in pan for 5 minutes before removing to wire rack to cool. Makes 12 muffins.

*1 muffin: 236 Calories; 8.7 g Total Fat (4.2 g Mono, 0.8 g Poly, 3.2 g Sat); 42 mg Cholesterol; 36 g Carbohydrate; 1 g Fibre; 5 g Protein; 250 mg Sodium*

Pictured on page 85.

# Rummy Eggnog Muffins

| | | |
|---|---|---|
| All-purpose flour | 2 cups | 500 mL |
| Brown sugar, packed | 2/3 cup | 150 mL |
| Baking powder | 1 tbsp. | 15 mL |
| Salt | 1/2 tsp. | 2 mL |
| Ground nutmeg | 1/2 tsp. | 2 mL |
| Ground cinnamon | 1/4 tsp. | 1 mL |
| Eggnog (see Tip) | 3/4 cup | 175 mL |
| Dark (navy) rum | 1/2 cup | 125 mL |
| Butter (or hard margarine), melted | 1/3 cup | 75 mL |
| Large egg | 1 | 1 |
| Butter (or hard margarine), melted | 1 tsp. | 5 mL |

Measure first 6 ingredients into large bowl. Stir. Make a well in centre.

Beat next 4 ingredients in small bowl. Add to well. Stir until just moistened. Fill 12 greased muffin cups 3/4 full.

Combine butter and gingersnap crumbs in small bowl. Sprinkle over batter. Bake in 375°F (190°C) oven for 18 to 20 minutes until wooden pick inserted in centre comes out clean. Let stand in pan for 5 minutes before removing to wire rack to cool. Makes 12 muffins.

*1 muffin: 231 Calories; 7.5 g Total Fat (2.2 g Mono, 0.4 g Poly, 4.4 g Sat); 39 mg Cholesterol; 33 g Carbohydrate; trace Fibre; 3 g Protein; 250 mg Sodium*

Pictured on page 85.

*Full of holiday cheer, rum and eggnog are an unbeatable combo. This traditional pairing is together again in a moist, tender muffin. These also work great as mini-muffins for bite-sized holiday treats.*

### tip

When eggnog is not available, use 3/4 cup (175 mL) buttermilk and 1/4 tsp. (1 mL) ground nutmeg instead.

*With flavours similar to a hot cross bun, these muffins are sure to be popular at any holiday breakfast or brunch. Try the Hot Cross Muffin variation for an extra-special touch.*

### hot cross muffins

Want to turn your Spiced Fruit Muffins into hot cross muffins? Simply stir 2 tsp. (10 mL) milk and 1/8 tsp. (0.5 mL) vanilla extract into 1/2 cup (125 mL) icing (confectioner's) sugar until smooth. Spoon into a piping bag fitted with a small tip or a resealable freezer bag with a tiny piece snipped off 1 corner. Pipe crosses onto cooled muffins.

# Spiced Fruit Muffins

| | | |
|---|---|---|
| All-purpose flour | 2 cups | 500 mL |
| Granulated sugar | 1/3 cup | 75 mL |
| Baking powder | 1 tbsp. | 15 mL |
| Ground cinnamon | 1/2 tsp. | 2 mL |
| Salt | 1/2 tsp. | 2 mL |
| Ground allspice | 1/8 tsp. | 0.5 mL |
| Ground nutmeg | 1/8 tsp. | 0.5 mL |
| Large egg | 1 | 1 |
| Milk | 1 cup | 250 mL |
| Cooking oil | 1/3 cup | 75 mL |
| Chopped mixed glazed fruit | 1/2 cup | 125 mL |
| Currants (or dark raisins) | 1/2 cup | 125 mL |

Measure first 7 ingredients into large bowl. Stir. Make a well in centre.

Beat next 3 ingredients in medium bowl. Add to well.

Add glazed fruit and currants. Stir until just moistened. Fill 12 greased muffin cups 3/4 full. Bake in 375°F (190°C) oven for 18 to 20 minutes until wooden pick inserted in centre of muffin comes out clean. Let stand in pan for 5 minutes before removing to wire rack to cool. Makes 12 muffins.

*1 muffin: 199 Calories; 6.7 g Total Fat (3.8 g Mono, 1.9 g Poly, 0.7 g Sat); 17 mg Cholesterol; 32 g Carbohydrate; 1 g Fibre; 3 g Protein; 186 mg Sodium*

Pictured below.

# Marmalade Ginger Crowns

**PASTRY**

| | | |
|---|---|---|
| All-purpose flour | 2 cups | 500 mL |
| Minced crystallized ginger | 3 tbsp. | 50 mL |
| Granulated sugar | 2 tbsp. | 30 mL |
| Baking powder | 1 tbsp. | 15 mL |
| Salt | 1/2 tsp. | 2 mL |
| Baking soda | 1/4 tsp. | 1 mL |
| Cold butter (or hard margarine), cut up | 1/3 cup | 75 mL |
| Sour cream | 1/2 cup | 125 mL |
| Vanilla extract | 1/2 tsp. | 2 mL |
| Large egg | 1 | 1 |

**FILLING**

| | | |
|---|---|---|
| Block of cream cheese, softened | 4 oz. | 125 g |
| Orange marmalade | 1/4 cup | 60 mL |
| Minced crystallized ginger | 1 tbsp. | 15 mL |

*Crisp pastry crowns cradle a ginger-orange custard filling. Serve them warm and you may just be crowned queen (or king) of festive baking!*

**Pastry:** Combine first 6 ingredients in medium bowl. Stir. Cut in butter until mixture resembles coarse crumbs. Make a well in centre.

Combine remaining 3 ingredients in small bowl. Add to well. Stir until soft dough forms. Turn out onto lightly floured surface. Knead 8 times. Roll or pat out to 9 x 12 inch (22 x 30 cm) rectangle. Cut into twelve 3 inch (7.5 cm) squares. Press into bottom and sides of 12 greased muffin cups.

**Filling:** Combine all 3 ingredients in separate small bowl. Spoon about 1 tbsp. (15 mL) mixture into each lined muffin cup. Bake in 425°F (220°C) oven for about 15 minutes until pastry is golden. Let stand in pan for 10 minutes before removing to wire rack. Makes 12 crowns.

*1 crown: 210 Calories; 10.5 g Total Fat (2.9 g Mono, 0.4 g Poly, 6.5 g Sat); 43 mg Cholesterol; 26 g Carbohydrate; trace Fibre; 4 g Protein; 269 mg Sodium*

Pictured on page 91.

*These light, tender scones are perfect for a breakfast get-together. Best served hot with butter and jam.*

## variations

Turn your currant scones into fruit scones by using 1 cup (250 mL) glazed fruit instead of currants. Or add an orangey twist by adding 1 tbsp. (15 mL) grated orange zest along with the currants.

# Currant Scones

| | | |
|---|---|---|
| All-purpose flour | 2 cups | 500 mL |
| Granulated sugar | 1/4 cup | 60 mL |
| Baking powder | 4 tsp. | 20 mL |
| Salt | 1/2 tsp. | 2 mL |
| Cold butter (or hard margarine), cut up | 1/4 cup | 60 mL |
| Currants | 1/2 cup | 125 mL |
| Large egg, fork-beaten | 1 | 1 |
| Milk | 2/3 cup | 150 mL |
| Milk | 1 tbsp. | 15 mL |
| Granulated sugar | 1 tsp. | 5 mL |

Combine first 4 ingredients in large bowl. Cut in butter until mixture resembles coarse crumbs.

Add currants. Stir. Make a well in centre.

Combine egg and milk in small bowl. Add to well. Stir until soft dough forms. Turn out onto lightly floured surface. Knead 8 times. Divide dough in half. Roll or pat out each half to 6 inch (15 cm) circle. Transfer to greased baking sheet.

Brush tops with second amount of milk. Sprinkle with second amount of sugar. Score 6 wedges in each circle, about 1/2 inch (12 mm) deep, using sharp knife. Bake in 425°F (220°C) oven for about 15 minutes until golden and wooden pick inserted in centre comes out clean. Each scone cuts into 6 wedges, for a total of 12 wedges.

*1 wedge: 148 Calories; 4.4 g Total Fat (1.2 g Mono, 0.2 g Poly, 2.6 g Sat); 26 mg Cholesterol; 25 g Carbohydrate; 1 g Fibre; 3 g Protein; 224 mg Sodium*

Pictured at right.

1. Marmalade Ginger Crowns, page 89
2. Currant Scones, page 90
3. Orange Cranberry Wedges, page 91

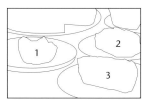

# Orange Cranberry Wedges

| | | |
|---|---|---|
| Biscuit mix | 2 cups | 500 mL |
| Orange-flavoured dried cranberries | 1 cup | 250 mL |
| Grated orange zest (see Tip, page 12) | 1 tbsp. | 15 mL |
| Orange juice | 1/3 cup | 75 mL |
| Vanilla-flavoured milk | 1/3 cup | 75 mL |

*Cranberry and orange, two favourite flavours of the season, combine for a truly fantastic biscuit. Using biscuit mix is an easy shortcut for a quick and convenient holiday treat.*

Combine first 3 ingredients in medium bowl. Make a well in centre.

Combine orange juice and milk in small bowl. Add to well. Stir until just moistened. Spread in greased 8 inch (20 cm) round pan. Bake in 350°F (175°C) oven for about 30 minutes until wooden pick inserted in centre comes out clean. Let stand in pan for 10 minutes before inverting onto wire rack. Cuts into 12 wedges.

*1 wedge: 204 Calories; 7.1 g Total Fat (3.0 g Mono, 0.6 g Poly, 2.0 g Sat); 1 mg Cholesterol; 32 g Carbohydrate; 1 g Fibre; 4 g Protein; 427 mg Sodium*

Pictured below.

*Love gingerbread? Enjoy those same spicy flavours for breakfast—without breaking into your stash of Christmas cookies! Serve these hot with lots of butter.*

**tip**

To make soured milk, measure 1 1/2 tsp. (7 mL) white vinegar or lemon juice into a 1 cup (250 mL) liquid measure. Add enough milk to make 1/2 cup (125 mL). Stir. Let stand for 5 minutes.

# Ginger Scones

| All-purpose flour | 2 cups | 500 mL |
| Granulated sugar | 1 tbsp. | 15 mL |
| Baking powder | 2 tsp. | 10 mL |
| Baking soda | 1/2 tsp. | 2 mL |
| Ground cinnamon | 1/2 tsp. | 2 mL |
| Ground ginger | 1/2 tsp. | 2 mL |
| Salt | 3/4 tsp. | 4 mL |
| Cold butter (or hard margarine), cut up | 1/4 cup | 60 mL |
| Buttermilk (or soured milk, see Tip) | 1/2 cup | 125 mL |
| Fancy (mild) molasses | 1/4 cup | 60 mL |
| Large egg, fork-beaten | 1 | 1 |
| Milk | 1 tbsp. | 15 mL |
| Granulated sugar | 1 tsp. | 5 mL |

Combine first 7 ingredients in large bowl. Cut in butter until mixture resembles coarse crumbs. Make a well in centre.

Add next 3 ingredients to well. Stir until soft dough forms. Turn out onto lightly floured surface. Knead 8 times. Divide dough in half. Roll or pat each half into a 6 inch (15 cm) circle. Place on greased baking sheet.

Brush tops with milk. Sprinkle with sugar. Score 6 wedges in each circle, about 1/2 inch (12 mm) deep, using sharp knife. Bake in 425°F (220°C) oven for about 15 minutes until golden and wooden pick inserted in centre comes out clean. Each scone cuts into 6 wedges, for a total of 12 wedges.

*1 wedge: 136 Calories; 4.3 g Total Fat (1.2 g Mono, 0.2 g Poly, 2.6 g Sat); 26 mg Cholesterol; 22 g Carbohydrate; trace Fibre; 3 g Protein; 288 mg Sodium*

Pictured at right.

# Cream Scones

| All-purpose flour | 4 cups | 1 L |
|---|---|---|
| Granulated sugar | 1/2 cup | 125 mL |
| Baking powder | 8 tsp. | 40 mL |
| Salt | 1 tsp. | 5 mL |
| Milk | 1 cup | 250 mL |
| Whipping cream | 1 cup | 250 mL |
| Large eggs, fork-beaten | 2 | 2 |
| Milk | 1 tbsp. | 15 mL |
| Granulated sugar | 1 tsp. | 5 mL |

Combine first 4 ingredients in large bowl. Make a well in centre.

Combine next 3 ingredients in small bowl. Add to well. Stir until soft dough forms. Turn out onto lightly floured surface. Knead 8 times. Roll or pat out to 1 inch (2.5 cm) thickness. Cut out circles with lightly floured 2 inch (5 cm) biscuit cutter. Arrange, about 1 inch (2.5 cm) apart, on greased baking sheet (see Tip).

Brush tops with second amount of milk. Sprinkle with second amount of sugar. Bake in 425°F (220°C) oven for about 15 minutes until golden. Makes about 24 scones.

*1 scone: 128 Calories; 4.0 g Total Fat (1.2 g Mono, 0.2 g Poly, 2.4 g Sat); 29 mg Cholesterol; 20 g Carbohydrate; trace Fibre; 3 g Protein; 198 mg Sodium*

Pictured below.

*Use up your leftover whipping cream for the richest, most tender scones you've ever had.*

**tip**

For softer-sided scones, arrange the circles close together on your baking sheet.

Left: Cream Scones, above
Right: Ginger Scones, page 92

Along with holiday festivities comes the traditional holiday flavours. Here, eggnog is paired with the popular flavours of orange, cranberry and spices. This treat may just become traditional holiday fare for your family!

# Orange Eggnog Loaf

| | | |
|---|---|---|
| All-purpose flour | 2 cups | 500 mL |
| Baking powder | 1 1/2 tsp. | 7 mL |
| Ground cinnamon | 1 tsp. | 5 mL |
| Baking soda | 1/2 tsp. | 2 mL |
| Salt | 1/2 tsp. | 2 mL |
| Eggnog (see Tip) | 1 cup | 250 mL |
| Grated orange zest | 2 tsp. | 10 mL |
| Dried cranberries | 1/2 cup | 125 mL |
| Butter (or hard margarine), softened | 1/3 cup | 75 mL |
| Granulated sugar | 2/3 cup | 150 mL |
| Large eggs | 2 | 2 |
| Icing (confectioner's) sugar | 3 tbsp. | 50 mL |
| Frozen concentrated orange juice, thawed | 2 tbsp. | 30 mL |

Measure first 5 ingredients into small bowl. Stir. Set aside.

Combine eggnog and orange zest in separate small bowl. Add cranberries. Stir well.

Cream butter and granulated sugar in medium bowl. Add eggs 1 at a time, beating well after each addition. Add flour mixture in 3 additions, alternating with eggnog mixture in 2 additions, stirring after each addition until just combined. Spread in greased 9 x 5 x 3 inch (22 x 12.5 x 7.5 cm) loaf pan. Bake in 350°F (175°C) oven for about 50 minutes until wooden pick inserted in centre comes out clean. Remove pan to wire rack.

Stir icing sugar and concentrated orange juice in separate small bowl until smooth. Brush on hot loaf. Let stand in pan for 10 minutes before removing to wire rack to cool. Cuts into 16 slices.

*1 slice: 167 Calories; 5.6 g Total Fat (1.6 g Mono, 0.3 g Poly, 3.3 g Sat); 43 mg Cholesterol; 27 g Carbohydrate; 1 g Fibre; 3 g Protein; 180 mg Sodium*

Pictured at right.

# Chocolate Banana Bread

| | | |
|---|---|---|
| Butter (or hard margarine), softened | 1/2 cup | 125 mL |
| Granulated sugar | 2/3 cup | 150 mL |
| Large eggs | 2 | 2 |

*(continued on next page)*

| | | |
|---|---|---|
| Mashed banana (about 3 medium) | 1 cup | 250 mL |
| Vanilla extract | 1 tsp. | 5 mL |
| | | |
| All-purpose flour | 2 cups | 500 mL |
| Mini semi-sweet chocolate chips | 1/2 cup | 125 mL |
| Cocoa, sifted if lumpy | 2 tbsp. | 30 mL |
| Baking powder | 1 tsp. | 5 mL |
| Baking soda | 1 tsp. | 5 mL |
| Salt | 1/2 tsp. | 2 mL |
| Chopped walnuts (optional) | 1/2 cup | 125 mL |

*Nothing draws them in like chocolate, especially in a fabulous banana loaf!*

Cream butter and sugar in large bowl. Add eggs 1 at a time, beating well after each addition.

Add banana and vanilla. Beat well.

Combine remaining 7 ingredients in medium bowl. Add to banana mixture. Stir until just moistened. Spread evenly in greased 9 x 5 x 3 inch (22 x 12.5 x 7.5 cm) loaf pan. Bake in 350°F (175°C) oven for about 1 hour until wooden pick inserted in centre comes out clean. Let stand in pan for 10 minutes before removing to wire rack to cool. Cuts into 16 slices.

*1 slice: 200 Calories; 8.6 g Total Fat (4.8 g Mono, 0.8 g Poly, 2.5 g Sat); 27 mg Cholesterol; 29 g Carbohydrate; 1 g Fibre; 3 g Protein; 257 mg Sodium*

Pictured below.

Top: Orange Eggnog Loaf, page 94
Bottom: Chocolate Banana Bread, page 94

*All the flavours of a traditional fruitcake in a speedy quickbread. Large pieces of fruit give a festive stained glass appearance to this rich loaf. To let the flavours mingle, make at least one day in advance.*

## tip

When toasting nuts, seeds or coconut, cooking times will vary for each type of nut—so never toast them together. For small amounts, place ingredient in an ungreased frying pan. Heat on medium for 3 to 5 minutes, stirring often, until golden. For larger amounts, spread ingredient evenly in an ungreased shallow pan. Bake in a 350°F (175°C) oven for 5 to 10 minutes, stirring or shaking often, until golden.

# Festive Fruit 'N' Nut Loaf

| | | |
|---|---|---|
| Brazil nuts, toasted (see Tip) | 1 1/3 cups | 325 mL |
| Whole pitted dates | 1 1/3 cups | 325 mL |
| Whole almonds | 1 cup | 250 mL |
| Green glazed cherries | 3/4 cup | 175 mL |
| Red glazed cherries | 3/4 cup | 175 mL |
| Chopped dried apricot (or peach), 1 inch (2.5 cm) pieces | 2/3 cup | 150 mL |
| Glazed pineapple rings, cut into 1 inch (2.5 cm) pieces | 2 | 2 |
| Large eggs | 2 | 2 |
| Brown sugar, packed | 2/3 cup | 150 mL |
| Butter (or hard margarine), softened | 1/3 cup | 75 mL |
| Spiced rum | 2 tbsp. | 30 mL |
| All-purpose flour | 1/2 cup | 125 mL |
| Baking powder | 1/4 tsp. | 1 mL |
| Baking soda | 1/4 tsp. | 1 mL |

Combine first 7 ingredients in extra-large bowl. Set aside.

Beat eggs in small bowl until thick and pale. Add next 3 ingredients. Beat well.

Combine remaining 3 ingredients in small bowl. Add to fruit mixture. Stir until well coated. Add egg mixture. Mix well. Line bottom and sides of greased 9 x 5 x 3 inch (22 x 12.5 x 7.5 cm) loaf pan with parchment (not waxed) paper. Spread batter in pan. Bake in 300°F (150°C) oven for about 2 hours until browned and firm. Remove pan to wire rack. Cover with foil. Let stand in pan for 10 minutes before removing to wire rack to cool completely. Remove and discard parchment paper. Wrap loaf with plastic wrap. Chill overnight. Cuts into 16 slices.

*1 slice:* 339 Calories; 16.6 g Total Fat (6.7 g Mono, 4.1 g Poly, 4.8 g Sat); 33 mg Cholesterol; 45 g Carbohydrate; 3 g Fibre; 5 g Protein; 82 mg Sodium

Pictured on page 99.

# Mincemeat Nut Bread

| | | |
|---|---|---|
| All-purpose flour | 2 cups | 500 mL |
| Ground cinnamon | 1 1/2 tsp. | 7 mL |
| Baking powder | 1 tsp. | 5 mL |
| Baking soda | 1 tsp. | 5 mL |
| Salt | 1/2 tsp. | 2 mL |
| Butter (or hard margarine), softened | 2/3 cup | 150 mL |
| Granulated sugar | 1 cup | 250 mL |
| Large eggs | 2 | 2 |
| Canned pure pumpkin (no spices), see Tip | 1 cup | 250 mL |
| Mincemeat | 1 cup | 250 mL |
| Coarsely chopped walnuts | 3/4 cup | 175 mL |

Combine first 5 ingredients in large bowl. Make a well in centre. Set aside.

Cream butter and sugar in medium bowl. Add eggs, 1 at a time, beating well after each addition.

Add remaining 3 ingredients. Stir. Add to well. Stir until just moistened. Spread in greased 9 x 5 x 3 inch (22 x 12.5 x 7.5 cm) loaf pan. Bake in 350°F (175°C) oven for about 1 hour until wooden pick inserted in centre comes out clean. Let stand in pan for 10 minutes before removing to wire rack to cool. Cuts into 16 slices.

*1 slice: 249 Calories; 12.9 g Total Fat (3.1 g Mono, 3.1 g Poly, 5.9 g Sat); 44 mg Cholesterol; 32 g Carbohydrate; 1 g Fibre; 3 g Protein; 233 mg Sodium*

Pictured on page 99.

*If mincemeat is your holiday vice—or even if you've never had mincemeat before—this moist loaf is surely one to try. Pumpkin and spice add a unique twist, and walnuts add lots of crunch.*

### tip

Store any leftover pumpkin in an airtight container in the refrigerator for 3 to 5 days or in the freezer for up to 12 months.

*Do you go nuts for candied fruit and almonds? This pretty, light-coloured loaf has everything you're looking for!*

# Fruit And Nut Loaf

| | | |
|---|---|---|
| Butter (or hard margarine), softened | 1/2 cup | 125 mL |
| Granulated sugar | 1 cup | 250 mL |
| Large eggs | 2 | 2 |
| Milk | 1 cup | 250 mL |
| Vanilla extract | 1 tsp. | 5 mL |
| Almond extract | 1/2 tsp. | 2 mL |
| All-purpose flour | 2 1/8 cups | 530 mL |
| Chopped mixed glazed fruit | 3/4 cup | 175 mL |
| Raisins (or currants) | 3/4 cup | 175 mL |
| Chopped almonds | 1/2 cup | 125 mL |
| Baking powder | 2 tsp. | 10 mL |
| Salt | 1/2 tsp. | 2 mL |

Cream butter and sugar in medium bowl. Add eggs, 1 at a time, beating well after each addition.

Add next 3 ingredients. Stir.

Combine remaining 6 ingredients in large bowl. Add butter mixture. Stir until just moistened. Spread in greased 9 x 5 x 3 inch (22 x 12.5 x 7.5 cm) loaf pan. Bake in 350°F (175°C) oven for about 1 hour until wooden pick inserted in centre comes out clean. Let stand in pan for 10 minutes before removing to wire rack to cool. Cuts into 16 slices.

*1 slice: 245 Calories; 8.7 g Total Fat (3.2 g Mono, 0.9 g Poly, 4.1 g Sat); 39 mg Cholesterol; 39 g Carbohydrate; 1 g Fibre; 4 g Protein; 172 mg Sodium*

Pictured at right.

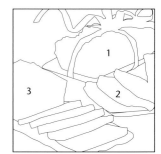

1. Festive Fruit 'N' Nut Loaf, page 96
2. Mincemeat Nut Bread, page 97
3. Fruit And Nut Loaf, above

*Though this ring may not be made of gold, it's still worthy of your finest holiday get-together. A fancy treat, this fluffy biscuit ring contains a surprise filling of fruit, nuts and cream cheese.*

## Cream Cheese Tea Ring

| | | |
|---|---|---|
| Block of cream cheese, softened | 8 oz. | 250 g |
| Granulated sugar | 1/4 cup | 60 mL |
| Vanilla extract | 1/2 tsp. | 2 mL |
| All-purpose flour | 2 cups | 500 mL |
| Granulated sugar | 2 tbsp. | 30 mL |
| Baking powder | 4 tsp. | 20 mL |
| Salt | 3/4 tsp. | 4 mL |
| Cold butter (or hard margarine), cut up | 1/4 cup | 60 mL |
| Milk, approximately | 3/4 cup | 175 mL |
| Chopped pecans (or walnuts or almonds) | 1/3 cup | 75 mL |
| Chopped raisins | 1/3 cup | 75 mL |
| Chopped red glazed cherries | 1/3 cup | 75 mL |
| ALMOND GLAZE | | |
| Icing (confectioner's) sugar | 1/2 cup | 125 mL |
| Almond extract | 1/4 tsp. | 1 mL |
| Milk, approximately | 1 tbsp. | 15 mL |
| Chopped pecans (or walnuts or almonds), toasted (see Tip, page 96), optional | 1 tbsp. | 15 mL |

Beat first 3 ingredients in small bowl until smooth. Set aside.

Combine next 4 ingredients in large bowl. Cut in butter until mixture resembles coarse crumbs.

Stir, adding milk until soft dough forms. Turn out onto lightly floured surface. Roll out to 10 x 14 inch (25 x 35 cm) rectangle. Spread with cream cheese mixture, leaving 3/4 inch (2 cm) edge.

Sprinkle next 3 ingredients over cream cheese mixture. Roll up, jelly roll-style, from long side. Press seam against roll to seal. Shape into ring. Place, seam-side down, on greased baking sheet. Pinch ends together to seal. Cut ring 14 times from outside edge to within 1 inch (2.5 cm) of centre using scissors (see photo 1). Turn each wedge on its side, all in the same direction, allowing them to overlap (see photo 2). Bake in 425°F (220°C) oven for 15 to 20 minutes until golden brown. Let stand on baking sheet on wire rack for about 30 minutes until cool.

*(continued on next page)*

**Almond Glaze:** Combine icing sugar and almond extract in small bowl. Stir, adding enough milk until smooth, barely pourable consistency. Makes about 1/4 cup (60 mL) glaze. Drizzle or pipe over tea ring.

Sprinkle with pecans. Cuts into 14 pieces.

*1 piece: 229 Calories; 11.1 g Total Fat (3.6 g Mono, 0.9 g Poly, 5.9 g Sat); 27 mg Cholesterol; 29 g Carbohydrate; 1 g Fibre; 4 g Protein; 281 mg Sodium*

Pictured below.

*Worth traveling to Denmark for—but easy enough to make in your own kitchen! These pretty little pastries can be changed up with your favourite flavours of jam or jelly.*

### variation

Use your favourite flavour of thick jam or jelly instead of lemon curd. Or, for a festive snowy look, after the pastries have cooled, dust with icing sugar.

### cream cheese danish pastries

Place a 1/2 inch (12 mm) cube of cream cheese in the centre of each dent before adding lemon curd.

# Danish Pastries

| | | |
|---|---|---|
| Warm water | 1/4 cup | 60 mL |
| Granulated sugar | 1 tsp. | 5 mL |
| Envelope of active dry yeast (or 2 1/4 tsp., 11 mL) | 1/4 oz. | 8 g |
| All-purpose flour | 4 cups | 1 L |
| Granulated sugar | 1/4 cup | 60 mL |
| Salt | 1 tsp. | 5 mL |
| Cold butter (or hard margarine), cut up | 1 1/4 cups | 300 mL |
| Milk | 1 cup | 250 mL |
| Large eggs, fork-beaten | 2 | 2 |
| Large egg, fork-beaten | 1 | 1 |
| Lemon curd | 16 tsp. | 80 mL |
| Finely chopped walnuts (or pecans) | 1/3 cup | 75 mL |

Stir warm water and sugar in small bowl until sugar is dissolved. Sprinkle yeast over top. Let stand for 10 minutes. Stir until yeast is dissolved.

Combine next 3 ingredients in large bowl. Cut in butter until mixture resembles coarse crumbs.

Pour milk into small saucepan. Heat and stir on medium until very hot and bubbles form around edge of saucepan. Transfer to separate small bowl. Let stand for 5 minutes to cool slightly.

Slowly add first amount of eggs, stirring constantly. Add yeast mixture. Stir. Add to flour mixture, mixing until soft dough forms. Place in separate greased large bowl, turning once to grease top. Cover with greased waxed paper and tea towel. Refrigerate for at least 6 hours or overnight.

Divide dough into 2 portions. Roll out 1 portion on lightly floured surface to 8 x 16 inch (20 x 40 cm) rectangle, about 1/2 inch (12 mm) thick. Cut into 4 inch (10 cm) squares. Fold corners of each square almost to centre. Press down in centre to make a dent. Arrange, about 2 inches (5 cm) apart, on greased baking sheet. Brush with second amount of egg. Repeat with remaining portion of dough.

*(continued on next page)*

Spoon 1 tsp. (5 mL) lemon curd into each dent. Sprinkle with walnuts. Cover with greased waxed paper and tea towel. Let stand for 15 minutes. Bake in 400°F (205°C) oven for about 20 minutes until golden. Makes 16 pastries.

*1 pastry: 296 Calories; 17.3 g Total Fat (4.5 g Mono, 1.9 g Poly, 9.6 g Sat); 81 mg Cholesterol; 31 g Carbohydrate; 1 g Fibre; 6 g Protein; 271 mg Sodium*

Pictured below.

*Just as good for gift-giving as they are for serving guests at a holiday tea party. A nice blend of spices makes for a truly festive flavour. If you do give these as a gift, simply put them in a decorative tin, topped with a bow.*

## about molasses

What makes molasses so sugary-sweet? Perhaps it's because molasses is formed as white sugar is refined from sugarcane syrup. Although it may not look very tasty, its dark, caramelized flavour is an indispensable ingredient in gingerbread and other foods. Molasses come in three varieties— light, which can be served on pancakes and waffles, dark, which is often used in baking, and blackstrap, which is much more thick and bitter.

# Gingerbread Pull-Aparts

| | | |
|---|---|---|
| Warm water | 1/2 cup | 125 mL |
| Granulated sugar | 1 tsp. | 5 mL |
| Envelope of active dry yeast (or 2 1/4 tsp., 11 mL) | 1/4 oz. | 8 g |
| Brown sugar, packed | 1/4 cup | 60 mL |
| Fancy (mild) molasses | 2 tbsp. | 30 mL |
| Milk | 2 tbsp. | 30 mL |
| Butter (or hard margarine) | 1 1/2 tbsp. | 25 mL |
| Salt | 3/4 tsp. | 4 mL |
| All-purpose flour | 1 1/2 cups | 375 mL |
| Ground ginger | 1 1/2 tsp. | 7 mL |
| Ground cinnamon | 1/2 tsp. | 2 mL |
| Ground cloves | 1/4 tsp. | 1 mL |
| Large egg, fork-beaten | 1 | 1 |
| All-purpose flour | 1 1/4 cups | 300 mL |
| All-purpose flour, approximately | 1/4 cup | 60 mL |
| Butter (or hard margarine), melted | 1 1/2 tsp. | 7 mL |

Stir warm water and granulated sugar in medium bowl until sugar is dissolved. Sprinkle yeast over top. Let stand for 10 minutes. Stir until yeast is dissolved.

Combine next 5 ingredients in small saucepan. Heat and stir on medium for about 2 minutes until butter is melted and brown sugar is dissolved. Remove from heat. Let stand for 5 minutes to cool slightly. Add to yeast mixture. Stir well.

Combine next 4 ingredients in large bowl. Make a well in centre.

Add egg and yeast mixture to well. Stir until smooth.

Work in second amount of flour, 1/4 cup (60 mL) at a time, mixing until soft dough forms.

*(continued on next page)*

Turn out dough onto lightly floured surface. Knead for 5 to 10 minutes until smooth and elastic, adding third amount of flour, 1 tbsp. (15 mL) at a time, if necessary, to prevent sticking. Place in greased large bowl, turning once to grease top. Cover with greased waxed paper and tea towel. Let stand in oven with light on and door closed for about 1 1/2 hours until doubled in bulk. Punch dough down. Turn out onto lightly floured surface. Knead for about 1 minute until smooth. Divide dough into 12 equal portions. Roll each portion into ball. Arrange in single layer in greased 9 inch (22 cm) round pan. Cover with greased waxed paper and tea towel. Let stand in oven with light on and door closed for about 45 minutes until doubled in size. Bake in 375°F (190°C) oven for about 20 minutes until golden brown and hollow sounding when tapped. Remove from oven.

Immediately brush tops of rolls with second amount of butter. Let stand in pan for 5 minutes before removing to wire rack to cool. Makes 12 pull-aparts.

*1 pull-apart: 154 Calories; 2.4 g Total Fat (0.7 g Mono, 0.1 g Poly, 1.4 g Sat); 21 mg Cholesterol; 30 g Carbohydrate; 1 g Fibre; 4 g Protein; 170 mg Sodium*

Pictured below.

*These are great to have on hand for any unexpected visitors! Bake up a couple batches ahead of time and keep them in the freezer for all your holiday season get-togethers.*

# Easy Overnight Buns

| | | |
|---|---|---|
| All-purpose flour | 2 cups | 500 mL |
| Cold water | 2 cups | 500 mL |
| Butter (or hard margarine), softened | 1/2 cup | 125 mL |
| Granulated sugar | 1/2 cup | 125 mL |
| Salt | 1 tsp. | 2 mL |
| Baking powder | 1/2 tsp. | 2 mL |
| Envelope of active dry yeast (or 2 1/4 tsp., 11 mL) | 1/4 oz. | 8 g |
| All-purpose flour, approximately | 4 cups | 1 L |

Beat first 7 ingredients in large bowl on low until moistened. Beat on medium-high for about 1 minute until well combined.

Work in second amount of flour, 1 cup (250 mL) at a time, until stiff dough forms. Place in greased large bowl, turning once to grease top. Cover with greased waxed paper and tea towel. Let stand at room temperature for at least 8 hours or overnight. Punch dough down. Divide into 4 portions. Divide each portion into 5 pieces, for a total of 20 pieces. Roll each piece into ball. Arrange balls, 1 inch (2.5 cm) apart, on greased baking sheet. Cover with greased waxed paper and tea towel. Let stand in oven with light on and door closed for about 1 1/2 hours until doubled in size. Bake in 375°F (190°C) oven for about 30 minutes until golden. Let stand on baking sheet for 10 minutes. Remove buns from baking sheet and place on wire racks to cool. Makes 20 buns.

*1 bun: 180 Calories; 4.6 g Total Fat (1.2 g Mono, 0.2 g Poly, 2.9 g Sat); 12 mg Cholesterol; 31 g Carbohydrate; 1 g Fibre; 4 g Protein; 156 mg Sodium*

*You're sure to be on Santa's knotty list this year—if you indulge in too many of these cinnamon treats. But, here's a secret: these whole-wheat cinnamon buns are actually not as sinful as you might think!*

# Knotty Cinnamon Buns

| | | |
|---|---|---|
| Butter (or hard margarine) | 2 tbsp. | 30 mL |
| Granulated sugar | 1 1/2 tbsp. | 25 mL |
| Salt | 1 tsp. | 5 mL |
| Hot water | 1 cup | 250 mL |
| Warm water | 1/4 cup | 60 mL |

*(continued on next page)*

| Granulated sugar | 1 tbsp. | 15 mL |
| Envelope of active dry yeast | 1/4 oz. | 8 g |
| (or 2 1/4 tsp, 11 mL) | | |
| Whole-wheat flour | 1 1/2 cups | 375 mL |
| All-purpose flour | 2 1/4 cups | 550 mL |
| Large egg, fork-beaten | 1 | 1 |
| Granulated sugar | 1/2 cup | 125 mL |
| Ground cinnamon | 3/4 tsp. | 4 mL |
| Butter (or hard margarine), melted | 3 tbsp. | 50 mL |

Combine first 3 ingredients in large bowl. Add hot water. Stir until butter is melted. Cool to room temperature.

Stir warm water and second amount of sugar in small bowl until sugar is dissolved. Sprinkle yeast over top. Let stand for 10 minutes. Stir until yeast is dissolved.

Add whole-wheat flour to butter mixture. Beat until smooth.

Add all-purpose flour, egg and yeast mixture. Mix until soft dough forms. Turn out onto lightly floured surface. Knead for 5 to 10 minutes until smooth and elastic. Place in greased extra-large bowl, turning once to grease top. Cover with greased waxed paper and tea towel. Let stand in oven with light on and door closed for about 1 hour until doubled in bulk. Punch dough down. Turn out onto lightly floured surface. Divide into 12 equal portions. Roll 1 portion into 10 inch (25 cm) long rope.

Combine third amount of sugar and cinnamon on plate. Brush rope with melted butter. Press into sugar mixture until coated. Form into simple knot. Place in greased 9 x 13 inch (22 x 33 cm) pan. Repeat with remaining dough, butter and sugar mixture. Cover with greased waxed paper and tea towel. Let stand in oven with light on and door closed for about 30 minutes until doubled in size. Bake in 375°F (190°C) oven for about 30 minutes until golden brown. Makes 12 buns.

*1 bun: 217 Calories; 5.5 g Total Fat (1.5 g Mono, 0.4 g Poly, 3.2 g Sat); 28 mg Cholesterol; 38 g Carbohydrate; 2 g Fibre; 5 g Protein; 235 mg Sodium*

Pictured on page 109.

*Cinnamon buns—with a chocolate twist! Using frozen bread dough makes these quick and easy to prepare, so you'll have more time to spend with friends and family.*

# Chocolate-Filled Rolls

| | | |
|---|---|---|
| Loaf of frozen white bread dough, covered and thawed in refrigerator overnight | 1 | 1 |
| Brown sugar, packed | 1/4 cup | 60 mL |
| Cocoa, sifted if lumpy | 1 tbsp. | 15 mL |
| Ground cinnamon | 1 tsp. | 5 mL |
| Mini semi-sweet chocolate chips | 3/4 cup | 175 mL |
| Finely chopped pecans (or walnuts) | 1/2 cup | 125 mL |
| **GLAZE** | | |
| Icing (confectioner's) sugar | 2/3 cup | 150 mL |
| Milk | 4 tsp. | 20 mL |
| Cocoa, sifted if lumpy | 2 tsp. | 10 mL |
| Vanilla extract | 1/8 tsp. | 0.5 mL |

Roll out dough on lightly floured surface to 12 x 14 inch (30 x 35 cm) rectangle. Brush with melted butter.

Combine next 3 ingredients in small bowl. Sprinkle over butter.

Sprinkle chocolate chips and pecans over brown sugar mixture. Press down lightly. Roll up from short side, jelly roll-style. Press seam against roll to seal. Cut into 1 inch (2.5 cm) slices. Arrange, cut-side up, about 1/2 inch (12 mm) apart in greased 9 x 13 inch (22 x 33 cm) pan. Cover with greased waxed paper and tea towel. Let stand in oven with light on and door closed for about 1 1/2 hours until doubled in size. Bake in 350°F (175°C) oven for about 25 minutes until golden. Let stand in pan on wire rack for about 10 minutes until slightly cooled.

**Glaze:** Combine all 4 ingredients in small bowl, adding more milk or icing sugar if necessary, until barely pourable consistency. Drizzle over each roll in pan. Makes 12 rolls.

*1 roll: 249 Calories; 9.7 g Total Fat (3.5 g Mono, 1.2 g Poly, 3.1 g Sat); 4 mg Cholesterol; 37 g Carbohydrate; 3 g Fibre; 5 g Protein; 226 mg Sodium*

Pictured at right.

1. Knotty Cinnamon Buns, page 106
2. Chocolate-Filled Rolls, page 108
3. Freezer Almond Cranberry Buns, page 110

*Everyone loves the scent of freshly baked sticky buns—but who has the time during the holidays? This recipe allows you to do all the prep work a month in advance so all you have to do is thaw these in the fridge overnight before popping them in the oven to bake.*

# Freezer Almond Cranberry Buns

| | | |
|---|---|---|
| Milk | 1/2 cup | 125 mL |
| Granulated sugar | 1/4 cup | 60 mL |
| Butter (or hard margarine) | 2 tbsp. | 30 mL |
| Salt | 1/4 tsp. | 1 mL |
| Warm water | 1 cup | 250 mL |
| All-purpose flour | 2 1/2 cups | 625 mL |
| Envelope of instant yeast | 1/4 oz. | 8 g |
| (or 2 1/4 tsp., 11 mL) | | |
| Ground nutmeg | 1/4 tsp. | 1 mL |
| All-purpose flour | 3/4 cup | 175 mL |
| All-purpose flour, approximately | 2 tbsp. | 30 mL |
| **FILLING** | | |
| Brown sugar, packed | 1/3 cup | 75 mL |
| Butter (or hard margarine), softened | 1/3 cup | 75 mL |
| Ground almonds | 1/3 cup | 75 mL |
| All-purpose flour | 2 tbsp. | 30 mL |
| Large egg, fork-beaten | 1 | 1 |
| Almond extract | 2 tsp. | 10 mL |
| Dried cranberries | 1 cup | 250 mL |
| Slivered almonds | 2/3 cup | 150 mL |
| **GLAZE** | | |
| Butter (or hard margarine) | 1/4 cup | 60 mL |
| Brown sugar, packed | 1/4 cup | 60 mL |
| Maple (or maple-flavoured) syrup | 2 tbsp. | 30 mL |

Combine first 4 ingredients in small saucepan. Heat and stir on medium until butter is melted and sugar is dissolved. Remove from heat.

Add warm water. Stir. Set aside.

Combine next 3 ingredients in large bowl. Make a well in centre. Add milk mixture. Stir well.

*(continued on next page)*

Work in second amount of flour, 1/4 cup (60 mL) at a time, until soft dough forms. Turn out onto lightly floured surface. Knead for 5 to 10 minutes until smooth and elastic, adding third amount of flour, 1 tbsp. (15 mL) at a time, if necessary, to prevent sticking. Place in separate greased large bowl, turning once to grease top. Cover with greased waxed paper and tea towel. Let stand in oven with light on and door closed for 30 minutes. Punch down dough. Turn out onto lightly floured surface. Knead for about 1 minute until smooth. Roll out to 9 x 14 inch (22 x 35 cm) rectangle.

**Filling:** Beat first 4 ingredients in medium bowl until well combined. Add egg and extract. Beat until smooth. Spread filling on dough rectangle, leaving 1 inch (2.5 cm) edge on 1 long side.

Sprinkle cranberries and second amount of almonds over filling. Press down lightly. Roll up from covered long side, jelly-roll style. Press seam against roll to seal.

**Glaze:** Combine all 3 ingredients in medium microwave-safe bowl. Microwave, covered, on high (100%) for about 45 seconds until butter is melted. Stir well. Spread glaze in greased 9 x 13 inch (22 x 33 cm) pan lined with parchment paper (see Note). Cut roll into 12 equal slices using floured knife. Arrange, cut-side up, over glaze in pan. Cover tightly with greased plastic wrap and foil. Freeze immediately. When ready to thaw, remove foil. Thaw in refrigerator for at least 8 hours or overnight. Let stand at room temperature for 1 hour. Bake, uncovered, in 350°F (175°C) oven for about 40 minutes until golden. Let stand in pan for 5 minutes before serving. Makes 12 buns.

*1 bun: 382 Calories; 16.6 g Total Fat (6.4 g Mono, 1.7 g Poly, 7.4 g Sat); 45 mg Cholesterol; 54 g Carbohydrate; 2 g Fibre; 7 g Protein; 142 mg Sodium*

Pictured on page 109.

**Note:** Greasing the bottom and sides of the pan will help secure the parchment paper. Extend the parchment paper over both long sides for easy removal.

*This traditional Christmas yeast cake is perfect for holiday coffee breaks. A small piece is all you'll need to refresh after a long day of shopping, caroling or gift-wrapping.*

# Stollen

|  | | |
|---|---|---|
| Finely chopped mixed glazed fruit | 1 cup | 250 mL |
| Raisins | 1/2 cup | 125 mL |
| Slivered almonds | 1/2 cup | 125 mL |
| Finely chopped citron peel | 1/3 cup | 75 mL |
| All-purpose flour | 1/4 cup | 60 mL |
| Currants | 1/4 cup | 60 mL |
| Grated lemon zest | 1 tsp. | 5 mL |
| All-purpose flour | 2 cups | 500 mL |
| Granulated sugar | 1/2 cup | 125 mL |
| Salt | 1 1/2 tsp. | 7 mL |
| Envelopes of instant yeast (1/4 oz., 8 g, each), or 4 1/2 tsp., 22 mL | 2 | 2 |
| Milk | 1 1/4 cups | 300 mL |
| Butter (or hard margarine) | 1/2 cup | 125 mL |
| Vanilla extract | 1 tsp. | 5 mL |
| Ground cardamom | 1/4 tsp. | 1 mL |
| All-purpose flour, approximately | 1 1/2 cups | 375 mL |
| Icing (confectioner's) sugar, sprinkle | | |

Stir first 7 ingredients in medium bowl until coated with flour. Set aside.

Combine next 4 ingredients in large bowl.

Heat milk in small heavy saucepan on medium for about 10 minutes, stirring often, until very hot and bubbles form around edge of saucepan. Remove from heat.

Add next 3 ingredients. Stir to melt butter. Mixture should be very warm but not hot. Add to yeast mixture. Beat until smooth. Add fruit mixture. Stir.

Knead in third amount of flour, 1/4 cup (60 mL) at a time, until dough is firm but still tacky. Cover with greased waxed paper and tea towel. Let stand in oven with light on and door closed for about 2 hours until doubled in bulk. Divide dough in half. Roll out each half on lightly floured surface to 10 inch (25 cm) circle. Fold over lengthwise, keeping top edge 1 inch (2.5 cm) back from edge of bottom. Place on greased baking sheet. Cover with greased waxed paper and tea towel. Let stand in oven with light on and door closed for about 40 minutes until almost doubled in size. Bake in 375°F (190°C) oven for about 15 minutes until golden. Let stand in pan for 10 minutes. Remove loaves from baking sheet and place on wire racks to cool.

*(continued on next page)*

Dust with icing sugar. Makes 2 loaves. Each loaf cuts into 16 pieces, for a total of 32 pieces.

*1 piece: 139 Calories; 4.1 g Total Fat (1.5 g Mono, 0.4 g Poly, 2.0 g Sat); 8 mg Cholesterol; 24 g Carbohydrate; 1 g Fibre; 3 g Protein; 148 mg Sodium*

Pictured on front cover and page 115.

## Swirled Raisin Braid

| | | |
|---|---|---|
| Loaf of frozen white bread dough, covered, thawed in refrigerator overnight | 1 | 1 |
| Dark raisins | 1/4 cup | 60 mL |
| Cocoa, sifted if lumpy | 2 tbsp. | 30 mL |
| Fancy (mild) molasses | 1 tbsp. | 15 mL |
| Water | 1 tsp. | 5 mL |

Cut dough into 3 equal portions. Set 1 portion aside.

Combine remaining 3 ingredients and 1 tsp. (5 mL) water in medium bowl. Add 2 dough portions. Knead in bowl for about 3 minutes until dough is marbled with cocoa mixture. Divide in half. Roll into 12 inch (30 cm) long ropes with slightly tapered ends. Roll plain dough portion into 12 inch (30 cm) long rope. Lay ropes side by side, with plain rope in the middle, on work surface. Pinch ropes together at one end. Braid ropes. Pinch together at opposite end. Tuck ends under. Place on greased baking sheet. Cover with greased waxed paper and tea towel. Let stand in oven with light on and door closed for about 1 hour until almost doubled in size. Bake in 350°F (175°C) oven for about 25 minutes until golden and hollow sounding when tapped. Remove to wire rack to cool. Cuts into 20 slices.

*1 slice: 69 Calories; 1.0 g Total Fat (trace Mono, trace Poly, trace Sat); 0 mg Cholesterol; 13 g Carbohydrate; 1 g Fibre; 2 g Protein; 127 mg Sodium*

Pictured on page 115.

*Sometimes making food festive is as simple as putting in the effort to make it look special. This braided raisin bread has two colours for a unique appearance and a dark, rich taste of molasses and raisins.*

_If you never know what to do with the leftover yolks after separating your eggs, this bread is the solution you're looking for. A rich, lightly sweet yeast bread with fragrant orange and cranberry._

## about yeast

Ever wonder what it is about yeast that causes it to make bread rise? As the yeast ferments it converts the starch in flour into gases. The bubbles are trapped in the elastic dough, causing the dough to expand, or rise. As you bake the dough, the heat in the oven kills the yeast and leaves the little air bubbles in bread that give it its soft texture.

# Cranberry Pecan Bread

| | | |
|---|---|---|
| Warm water | 1/4 cup | 60 mL |
| Granulated sugar | 1 tsp. | 5 mL |
| Envelope of active dry yeast (or 2 1/4 tsp., 11 mL) | 1/4 oz. | 8 g |
| Egg yolks (large), fork-beaten | 4 | 4 |
| Butter (or hard margarine), melted | 3/4 cup | 175 mL |
| Milk | 3/4 cup | 175 mL |
| Granulated sugar | 1/4 cup | 60 mL |
| Grated orange zest | 1 tbsp. | 15 mL |
| Salt | 1 tsp. | 5 mL |
| All-purpose flour, approximately | 3 1/2 cups | 875 mL |
| Chopped pecans | 1/2 cup | 125 mL |
| Dried cranberries | 1/2 cup | 125 mL |

Combine warm water and sugar in small bowl. Stir until sugar is dissolved. Sprinkle yeast over top. Let stand for 10 minutes. Stir to dissolve yeast.

Combine next 6 ingredients in large bowl. Add yeast mixture. Stir well.

Add 1/2 cup (125 mL) flour. Stir. Work in enough remaining flour until dough pulls away from side of bowl and is no longer sticky. Turn out onto lightly floured surface. Knead for 8 to 10 minutes until smooth and elastic.

Add pecans and cranberries. Knead for about 2 minutes until well distributed. Transfer dough to large greased bowl, turning once to grease top. Cover with greased waxed paper and tea towel. Let stand in oven with light on and door closed for about 1 hour until doubled in bulk. Punch dough down. Roll into 27 inch (78 cm) long rope. Coil into greased 10 inch (25 cm) angel food tube pan. Cover with greased waxed paper and tea towel. Let stand in oven with light on and door closed for about 1 hour until doubled in size. Bake in 375°F (190°C) oven for 45 to 50 minutes until dark golden brown and hollow sounding when tapped. Let stand in pan for 10 minutes before removing to wire rack to cool. Cuts into 16 slices.

_1 slice: 233 Calories; 12.6 g Total Fat (4.3 g Mono, 1.3 g Poly, 6.1 g Sat); 71 mg Cholesterol; 27 g Carbohydrate; 1 g Fibre; 4 g Protein; 215 mg Sodium_

Pictured at right.

*This Italian yeast bread (pronounced pan-uh-TOH-nee), is just sweet enough to satisfy.*

## about panettone

Panettone is a sweet, cake-like bread traditionally made with nuts, candied fruit, anise and eggs. This Italian bread is usually baked in a tall, cylindrical pan, known as a panettone pan. It's traditionally served at special occasions like weddings, Easter and Christmas.

# Panettone

| | | |
|---|---|---|
| Dark raisins, coarsely chopped | 1/2 cup | 125 mL |
| Golden raisins | 1/2 cup | 125 mL |
| Chopped mixed glazed fruit | 1/3 cup | 75 mL |
| Dry sherry (or Marsala) | 1/3 cup | 75 mL |
| Milk | 1/2 cup | 125 mL |
| Granulated sugar | 1 tbsp. | 15 mL |
| Active dry yeast | 2 1/2 tbsp. | 37 mL |
| All-purpose flour | 5 cups | 1.25 L |
| Granulated sugar | 1/3 cup | 75 mL |
| Salt | 1 tsp. | 5 mL |
| Milk | 3/4 cup | 175 mL |
| Butter (or hard margarine) | 1/2 cup | 125 mL |
| Large eggs fork-beaten | 3 | 3 |
| Egg yolks (large), fork-beaten | 3 | 3 |
| Finely grated lemon zest | 2 tsp. | 10 mL |
| Vanilla extract | 1 tsp. | 5 mL |
| Large egg, fork-beaten | 1 | 1 |

Measure first 4 ingredients into small bowl. Stir. Let stand for 30 minutes.

Combine milk and sugar in small heavy saucepan on medium. Heat and stir until warm and sugar is dissolved. Pour into separate small bowl. Let stand for 5 minutes.

Sprinkle yeast over top. Let stand for 10 minutes. Stir until yeast is dissolved.

Combine next 3 ingredients in extra-large bowl. Make a well in centre. Add fruit mixture to well. Stir. Add yeast mixture. Stir well.

Combine second amount of milk and butter in same small heavy saucepan. Heat and stir on medium until butter is almost melted. Pour into separate small bowl. Stir until butter is melted. Let stand for 5 minutes to cool slightly.

*(continued on next page)*

Add warm milk mixture and next 4 ingredients to flour mixture. Mix until dough starts to pull away from side of bowl. Cover with greased waxed paper and tea towel. Let stand in oven with light on and door closed for about 30 minutes until doubled in bulk. Punch dough down. Turn out onto lightly floured surface. Knead for 3 to 5 minutes until smooth. Divide into 2 equal portions. Roll 1 portion into ball. Press in bottom of greased 8 inch (20 cm) springform pan. Repeat with remaining portion and separate greased springform pan. Cover each with greased waxed paper and tea towel. Let stand in oven with light on and door closed for 30 minutes until doubled in size.

Brush top of each loaf with second amount of egg. Bake in 350°F (175°C) oven for 40 to 50 minutes until golden brown and hollow sounding when tapped. Let stand in pans for 10 minutes before removing to wire racks to cool. Makes 2 loaves. Each loaf cuts into 12 slices, for a total of 24 slices.

*1 slice: 187 Calories; 5.5 g Total Fat (1.7 g Mono, 0.4 g Poly, 2.9 g Sat); 66 mg Cholesterol; 30 g Carbohydrate; 1 g Fibre; 5 g Protein; 147 mg Sodium*

Pictured below.

*Starting with frozen bread dough makes for the most convenient Christmas bread. An attractive spiral of fruit and a drizzle of glaze ensures no one will know you used a shortcut!*

## about currants

A lot of people confuse raisins and currants. This is understandable, given that dried currants are made from tiny grapes, so they're essentially just small raisins. Dried currants are most commonly used in baking. But don't expect to find any grapes in redcurrant or blackcurrant jelly—they're made from completely unrelated berries!

# Christmas Bread

| | | |
|---|---|---|
| Loaf of frozen white bread dough, covered and thawed in refrigerator overnight | 1 | 1 |
| Currants (or raisins) | 1/4 cup | 60 mL |
| Maraschino cherries, drained and quartered | 1/4 cup | 60 mL |
| Chopped mixed glazed fruit | 1 tbsp. | 15 mL |
| Ground cinnamon | 1/4 tsp. | 1 mL |
| Butter (or hard margarine), melted (optional) | 1 tsp. | 5 mL |
| **GLAZE** | | |
| Icing (confectioner's) sugar | 1/3 cup | 75 mL |
| Water | 1 1/4 tsp. | 6 mL |
| Slivered almonds, toasted (see Tip, page 96), for garnish | 2 tbsp. | 30 mL |

Roll out dough on lightly floured surface to 9 x 12 inch (22 x 30 cm) rectangle.

Scatter next 3 ingredients over dough. Sprinkle with cinnamon. Roll up, jelly roll-style, from short side. Put roll, seam-side down, into greased 9 x 5 x 3 inch (22 x 12.5 x 7.5 cm) loaf pan. Cover with greased waxed paper and tea towel. Let stand in oven with light on and door closed until doubled in size. Bake in 375°F (190°C) oven for about 30 minutes until golden. Let stand in pan for 5 minutes.

Brush with butter. Remove to wire rack to cool.

**Glaze:** Mix icing sugar with enough water until barely pourable consistency. Makes about 2 tbsp. (30 mL) glaze. Drizzle over loaf.

Immediately sprinkle with almonds. Cuts into 16 slices.

*1 slice: 106 Calories; 1.4 g Total Fat (0.1 g Mono, trace Poly, 0.2 g Sat); 1 mg Cholesterol; 21 g Carbohydrate; 1 g Fibre; 3 g Protein; 160 mg Sodium*

Pictured at right.

Freshly baked bread with fruit and raisins is sure to fill your home with warm and inviting scents. Great for a festive brunch or buffet. You can decorate this wreath further by drizzling with glaze (page 122), or by sprinkling with chopped walnuts or cherries.

# Table Bread Wreath

| | | |
|---|---|---|
| Warm water | 1 cup | 250 mL |
| Granulated sugar | 2 tsp. | 10 mL |
| Envelopes of active dry yeast (1/4 oz., 8 g each) or 4 1/2 tsp., 22 mL | 2 | 2 |
| Butter (or hard margarine), softened | 3/4 cup | 175 mL |
| Granulated sugar | 1/2 cup | 125 mL |
| Large eggs | 2 | 2 |
| Salt | 1 tsp. | 5 mL |
| All-purpose flour | 2 cups | 500 mL |
| Chopped mixed glazed fruit | 1 cup | 250 mL |
| Raisins | 1/2 cup | 125 mL |
| All-purpose flour, approximately | 2 3/4 cups | 675 mL |
| Large egg, fork-beaten | 1 | 1 |

Stir warm water and sugar in small bowl until sugar is dissolved. Sprinkle yeast over top. Let stand for 10 minutes. Stir.

Cream butter and second amount of sugar in large bowl. Add eggs, 1 at a time, beating well after each addition. Add salt, flour and yeast mixture. Beat on medium for about 2 minutes until smooth.

Add glazed fruit and raisins. Mix. Work in enough of second amount of flour, 1 cup (250 mL) at a time, until soft dough forms. Turn out onto lightly floured surface. Knead for 5 to 8 minutes until smooth and elastic. Put into large greased bowl, turning once to grease top. Cover with greased waxed paper and tea towel. Let stand in oven with light on and door closed for about 2 hours until doubled in bulk.

Punch dough down. Divide into 3 equal portions. Roll each portion on lightly floured surface to 24 inch (60 cm) rope. Lay ropes side by side on work surface. Pinch ropes together at one end. Braid ropes. Shape into wreath, joining ends and pinching together. Transfer to baking sheet. Cover with greased waxed paper and tea towel. Let stand in oven with light on and door closed for about 1 hour until doubled in size. Brush with egg. Bake in 375°F (190°C) oven for 40 to 45 minutes until golden and hollow sounding when tapped. Remove to wire rack to cool. Cuts into 24 pieces.

*1 piece: 192 Calories; 6.3 g Total Fat (1.8 g Mono, 0.3 g Poly, 3.8 g Sat); 38 mg Cholesterol; 31 g Carbohydrate; 1 g Fibre; 4 g Protein; 154 mg Sodium*

Pictured at right.

*Certainly not your typical Christmas tree—this one tastes delicious! A festive treat made of golden-brown rolls flavoured with cardamom and fruit.*

## make your own glaze

Add some festive flair to your Christmas Tree Buns by decorating them with glaze. Simply combine 1 1/2 cups (375 mL) icing (confectioner's) sugar with 2 1/2 tbsp. (37 mL) water and 1/2 tsp. (2 mL) vanilla extract in a small bowl. Add more water if necessary until your glaze is a barely pourable consistency.

# Christmas Tree Buns

| | | |
|---|---|---|
| Warm water | 1/4 cup | 60 mL |
| Granulated sugar | 1 tsp. | 5 mL |
| Envelope of active dry yeast (or 2 1/4 tsp, 11 mL) | 1/4 oz. | 8 g |
| Milk | 1 1/2 cups | 375 mL |
| Large egg, fork-beaten | 1 | 1 |
| Granulated sugar | 6 tbsp. | 100 mL |
| Butter (or hard margarine), melted | 1/4 cup | 60 mL |
| Salt | 1 tsp. | 5 mL |
| Ground cardamom | 1/4 tsp. | 1 mL |
| All-purpose flour | 3 cups | 750 mL |
| Chopped mixed glazed fruit | 1/2 cup | 125 mL |
| Sultana raisins | 1/2 cup | 125 mL |
| Currants (or dark raisins) | 1/4 cup | 60 mL |
| All-purpose flour, approximately | 2 1/2 cups | 625 mL |
| Red (or green) glazed cherries, for garnish | 1/4 cup | 60 mL |

Stir warm water and sugar in small bowl until sugar is dissolved. Sprinkle yeast over top. Let stand for 10 minutes. Stir until yeast is dissolved.

Pour milk into small saucepan. Heat and stir on medium for about 1 minute until very hot and bubbles form around edge of saucepan. Transfer to large bowl. Let stand for 5 minutes to cool slightly.

Add next 5 ingredients and yeast mixture. Stir. Add first amount of flour. Stir.

Add next 3 ingredients. Stir.

*(continued on next page)*

Work in second amount of flour, 1/2 cup (125 mL) at a time, until soft dough forms. Turn out dough onto lightly floured surface. Knead for 5 to 10 minutes until smooth and elastic. Place in greased large bowl, turning once to grease top. Cover with greased waxed paper and tea towel. Let stand in oven with light on and door closed for about 1 1/2 hours until doubled in bulk. Punch dough down. Divide dough into 38 equal portions. Roll each portion into ball. Arrange, almost touching, on 2 greased baking sheets in tree shapes. Let stand in oven with light on and door closed for about 1 hour until doubled in size. Bake in 350°F (175°C) oven for 30 to 40 minutes until golden. Let stand on baking sheets for 10 minutes. Remove trees from baking sheets and place on wire racks to cool.

Sprinkle with glazed cherries. Makes 38 buns.

*1 bun: 100 Calories; 1.5 g Total Fat (0.4 g Mono, 0.1 g Poly, 0.9 g Sat); 9 mg Cholesterol; 20 g Carbohydrate; 1 g Fibre; 2 g Protein; 80 mg Sodium*

Pictured below.

Throughout this book measurements are given in Conventional and Metric measure. To compensate for differences between the two measurements due to rounding, a full metric measure is not always used. The cup used is the standard 8 fluid ounce. Temperature is given in degrees Fahrenheit and Celsius. Baking pan measurements are in inches and centimetres as well as quarts and litres. An exact metric conversion is given on this page as well as the working equivalent (Metric Standard Measure).

## Pans

| Conventional – Inches | Metric – Centimetres |
|---|---|
| 8 × 8 inch | 20 × 20 cm |
| 9 × 9 inch | 22 × 22 cm |
| 9 × 13 inch | 22 × 33 cm |
| 10 × 15 inch | 25 × 38 cm |
| 11 × 17 inch | 28 × 43 cm |
| 8 × 2 inch round | 20 × 5 cm |
| 9 × 2 inch round | 22 × 5 cm |
| 10 × 4 1/2 inch tube | 25 × 11 cm |
| 8 × 4 × 3 inch loaf | 20 × 10 × 7.5 cm |
| 9 × 5 × 3 inch loaf | 22 × 12.5 × 7.5 cm |

## Oven Temperatures

| Fahrenheit (°F) | Celsius (°C) | Fahrenheit (°F) | Celsius (°C) |
|---|---|---|---|
| 175° | 80° | 350° | 175° |
| 200° | 95° | 375° | 190° |
| 225° | 110° | 400° | 205° |
| 250° | 120° | 425° | 220° |
| 275° | 140° | 450° | 230° |
| 300° | 150° | 475° | 240° |
| 325° | 160° | 500° | 260° |

## Spoons

| Conventional Measure | Metric Exact Conversion Millilitre (mL) | Metric Standard Measure Millilitre (mL) |
|---|---|---|
| 1/8 teaspoon (tsp.) | 0.6 mL | 0.5 mL |
| 1/4 teaspoon (tsp.) | 1.2 mL | 1 mL |
| 1/2 teaspoon (tsp.) | 2.4 mL | 2 mL |
| 1 teaspoon (tsp.) | 4.7 mL | 5 mL |
| 2 teaspoons (tsp.) | 9.4 mL | 10 mL |
| 1 tablespoon (tbsp.) | 14.2 mL | 15 mL |

## Cups

| | | |
|---|---|---|
| 1/4 cup (4 tbsp.) | 56.8 mL | 60 mL |
| 1/3 cup (5 1/3 tbsp.) | 75.6 mL | 75 mL |
| 1/2 cup (8 tbsp.) | 113.7 mL | 125 mL |
| 2/3 cup (10 2/3 tbsp.) | 151.2 mL | 150 mL |
| 3/4 cup (12 tbsp.) | 170.5 mL | 175 mL |
| 1 cup (16 tbsp.) | 227.3 mL | 250 mL |
| 4 1/2 cups | 1022.9 mL | 1000 mL(1 L) |

## Dry Measurements

| Conventional Measure Ounces (oz.) | Metric Exact Conversion Grams (g) | Metric Standard Measure Grams (g) |
|---|---|---|
| 1 oz. | 28.3 g | 28 g |
| 2 oz. | 56.7 g | 57 g |
| 3 oz. | 85.0 g | 85 g |
| 4 oz. | 113.4 g | 125 g |
| 5 oz. | 141.7 g | 140 g |
| 6 oz. | 170.1 g | 170 g |
| 7 oz. | 198.4 g | 200 g |
| 8 oz. | 226.8 g | 250 g |
| 16 oz. | 453.6 g | 500 g |
| 32 oz. | 907.2 g | 1000 g (1 kg) |

## Casseroles

| Canada & Britain | | United States | |
|---|---|---|---|
| Standard Size Casserole | Exact Metric Measure | Standard Size Casserole | Exact Metric Measure |
| 1 qt. (5 cups) | 1.13 L | 1 qt. (4 cups) | 900 mL |
| 1 1/2 qts. (7 1/2 cups) | 1.69 L | 1 1/2 qts. (6 cups) | 1.35 L |
| 2 qts. (10 cups) | 2.25 L | 2 qts. (8 cups) | 1.8 L |
| 2 1/2 qts. (12 1/2 cups) | 2.81 L | 2 1/2 qts. (10 cups) | 2.25 L |
| 3 qts. (15 cups) | 3.38 L | 3 qts. (12 cups) | 2.7 L |
| 4 qts. (20 cups) | 4.5 L | 4 qts. (16 cups) | 3.6 L |
| 5 qts. (25 cups) | 5.63 L | 5 qts. (20 cups) | 4.5 L |

# Tip Index

# Recipe Index

most loved recipe collection most loved recipe collection most loved recipe collection most loved recipe collection most loved recipe collection most loved recipe col ction most loved recipe collection most loved recipe collection most loved recipe col most loved recipe collection most loved recipe collection most loved recipe collection tion most loved recipe collection most loved recipe collection most loved recipe colle most loved recipe collection most loved recipe collection most loved recipe collection e collection most loved recipe collection most loved recipe collection most loved reci ction most loved recipe collection most loved recipe collection most loved recipe col most loved recipe collection most loved recipe collection most loved recipe collection loved recipe collection most loved recipe collection most loved recipe collection most ction most loved recipe collection most loved recipe collection most loved recipe col most loved recipe collection most loved recipe collection most loved recipe collection tion most loved recipe colle most loved recipe collection most loved recipe colle most loved recipe collection most loved recipe collection most loved recipe collection e collection most loved recipe collection most loved recipe collection most loved reci ction most loved recipe collection most loved recipe collection most loved recipe col most loved recipe collection most loved recipe collection most loved recipe collection loved recipe collection most loved recipe collection most loved recipe collection most ction most loved recipe collection most loved recipe collection most loved recipe col most loved recipe collection most loved recipe collection most loved recipe collection tion most loved recipe collection most loved recipe collection most loved recipe colle most loved recipe collection most loved recipe collection most loved recipe collection e collection most loved recipe collection most loved recipe collection most loved reci ction most loved recipe collection most loved recipe collection most loved recipe col most loved recipe collection most loved recipe collection most loved recipe collection loved recipe collection most loved recipe collection most loved recipe collection most ction most loved recipe collection most loved recipe collection most loved recipe col most loved recipe collection most loved recipe collection most loved recipe collectio tion most loved recipe collection most loved recipe collection most loved recipe colle most loved recipe collection most loved recipe collection most loved recipe collection e collection most loved recipe collection most loved recipe collection most loved rec